Praise for *Remembrance* . . .

"Sensitive mystic and spiritual teacher, Alejandra Warden, invites us into a richly descriptive and cellular journey back to our essential and shared nature, that of the "golden substance" of "primordial love" and Oneness. Guided by the ancestral feminine and the angelic, Alejandra serves as a conduit for a mythopoetic narrative of Earth's birthing, nonlinear knowing, embodiment, loss, and a call to remembrance. May we accept her beautiful gift of wisdom and listen deeply, particularly at this crucial time."

— Juliet Rohde-Brown Ph.D., author of *Imagine Forgiveness*, and Chair of Integrative Therapy and Healing Practices specialization of the Depth Psychology program, Pacifica Graduate Institute

"Alejandra is a highly respected leader and role model in both childhood education and spiritual development. Her book, *Remembrance*, offers us a vision of the evolution of human life on Earth grounded in a mature feminine wisdom. It is a story of the energetic power of love as a universal force behind the creation of all life. It is a story of how humanity has been created to mirror the universe to itself and how human beings are endowed with the capacity to rediscover the essence of love that is at the heart of their existence. With this rediscovery of who we really are, life on Earth is healed from the trauma of centuries of abuse."

— Edward W. Bastian, Ph.D., author of *InterSpiritual Meditation* and *Mandala: Creating an Authentic Spiritual Path*

"Open the door and journey into the multiple planes and passages of the cosmic order of existence through the eyes and experience of Alejandra Warden's mystical awakening. Piercing through the multiple layers of this manifest realm of beauty, pain, and suffering with fractal precision, Warden powerfully shares the intimate and sacred transmission she received . . . These timeless teachings of love, wisdom, and wholeness call us back into remembrance of the Ultimate Reality and the voice of the Divine Feminine, offering abundant hope and shining possibilities as we move through these difficult times toward rebirth into a new civilization of heaven on earth."

—Rev. Cynthia Brix and William Keepin, Ph.D., authors of *Divine Duality* and *Women Healing Women*

"As I finished reading *Remembrance*, I felt a deep peace laying over me and the land. Reading this book in the midst of today's climate of upheaval and anxiety is transformational. Seeing with the eyes of the heart, Alejandra Warden shares her vision, which includes us all. *Remembrance* is a portal into our true nature of love and interconnectedness with all life. Her ability to trace our evolution and history to the present is brilliant, and possibilities for the future, hopeful. In this transformational time on Earth, this book offers guidance and inspiration."

— Celeste Yacoboni, author of *How Do You Pray? Inspiring Responses from Religious Leaders, Spiritual Guides, Healers, Activists & Other Lovers of Humanity*

"With *Remembrance,* Alejandra Warden offers us a beautiful mystical vision that shines a luminous ray of hope in the darkness of these confusing times."

— Dave Waugh, author of *Evolving Soulfully: Cultivating Natural Vitality, Deep Presence, Intimacy, Meaning and Purpose*

"*Remembrance* is a shimmering aurora through the holy darkness, a precious medicine for our time, a jewel in an emerging field of wild feminine wisdom, a paradigm shift from which there is no going back."

— Vera de Chalambert, public theologian, spiritual storyteller

"In this soul-nourishing book, Alejandra Warden beautifully articulates the nature of the Divine Feminine—no easy task. And even more precious, by telling her story, the reader gets a window into how the Feminine communicates, that we may all be open to her when she comes knocking."

— Chris Maddox, founder of The Wild Woman Project

Remembrance

A Vision of the Sacred Feminine and the Renewal of the Earth

Alejandra Warden

Illustrated by
Julia Mandeville

Albion
Andalus
Boulder, Colorado
2022

*"The old shall be renewed,
and the new shall be made holy."*
— Rabbi Avraham Yitzhak Kook

Copyright © 2022 Alejandra Warden
First edition. All rights reserved.

No part of this book may be reproduced or transmitted in any form or by any means, electronic or mechanical, including photocopy, recording, or any information storage or retrieval system, except for brief passages in connection with a critical review, without permission in writing from the publisher:

Albion-Andalus, Inc.
P. O. Box 19852
Boulder, CO 80308
www.albionandalus.com

Design and composition by Albion-Andalus Books
Cover design by D.A.M. Cool Graphics
Illustrations by Julia Mandeville

ISBN-13: 978-1-953220-12-7 (Hardcover)
ISBN-13: 978-1-953220-20-2 (Paperback)

Manufactured in the United States of America

*To Walter and my kids,
the Earth,
Woman,
and the Feminine in All of Us.*

Contents

Acknowledgements   *xi*
Prologue   *xiii*

PART ONE:
Woman, Remember

Chapter One: *Beginnings*   3
Chapter Two: *The Desert*   7
Chapter Three: *The Cloud*   11
Chapter Four: *The Ageless Woman*   15

PART TWO:
The Journey

Chapter Five: *A New Earth*   19
Chapter Six: *Bearers of Remembrance*   25
Chapter Seven: *The Time of the Descent*   31

PART THREE:
The Passages
The First Passage: Creation

Chapter Eight: *The Mother*   43
Chapter Nine: *The Universe*   49
Chapter Ten: *Being*   55

The Second Passage: Transformation

Chapter Eleven: The *Waters of Life*   61
Chapter Twelve: *Liquid Love*   63

Chapter Thirteen: *Fear*   71
Chapter Fourteen: *The Queen of the Sky*   73
Chapter Fifteen: *Bliss*   77

The Third Passage: Interconnection

Chapter Sixteen: *A Secret Garden*   81
Chapter Seventeen: *Drops of the Great Soul*   85
Chapter Eighteen: *Magic Memory*   89

PART FOUR:
Awakening

Chapter Nineteen: *The Human Being*   93
Chapter Twenty: *The Fabric of Love*   99
Chapter Twenty-One: *The Path to Freedom*   105
Chapter Twenty-Two: *The Source*   107

PART FIVE:
Cycles

Chapter Twenty-Three: *The Story of Our World*   113
Chapter Twenty-Four: *Hope*   119
Chapter Twenty-Five: *Change of Course*   123
Chapter Twenty-Six: *Time to Come Back*   127

PART SIX:
The Doors of Memory

Chapter Twenty-Seven: *After the Visions*   133
Chapter Twenty-Eight: *The Rebirth of the Feminine*   141

Part Seven:
Teachings of a Feminine Spirituality

Love	147
The Care of the Earth	147
The Evolution of the Earth	148
The Present Moment	148
Angels	149
The Porous Layers of Existence	149
The Created and the Uncreated, The One and the Many	151

About the Author

Acknowledgements

This book would not have been completed without the editing assistance of Walter, my life companion, Jamelah Zidan, and Netanel Miles-Yépez, my publisher, as well as the support of my kids, and the encouragements of my spiritual guides and my friends. My eternal gratitude to all of them.

— A.W.

Prologue

"When the miraculous bursts into our path, it changes our destiny."

For three consecutive days I woke up hearing these words in my head. I didn't know that they prefigured what was about to happen. It was in the autumn of 1996, and I had recently become a mother. I was raising children and working. Like most people, I had projects, goals, prospects. Like many women, I also clearly perceived the cultural injustice against the feminine in our world, and often, when I was alone in silence, deep inside I sensed a profound pain—piercing, ancient, and ancestral. But it was 'just a feeling.' Then I experienced a series of intense mystical experiences that would forever transform my life.

For seven months, I would receive teachings and visions on the sacred essence of a feminine wisdom, a wisdom that lies dormant in the depths of us all.* The recovery of this wisdom gives back to the feminine (and to women, in particular) a true purpose and path to freedom.

On this incredible journey of consciousness, I learned about the history of the Earth—from her origin to the present— and was shown the wonders of different realms of nature and dimensions of existence. Before my eyes, the tremendous

---

* When I speak of the feminine, I am referring to a quality inherent in the whole of humanity, nature, and the universe, not something unique to one gender. And when I speak of the maternal role, I am referring to any person who fulfills this role, not the birth-mother alone.

Remembrance

love, power, and wisdom of the feminine was unveiled, as well as a marvelous possible future for our planet.

As the cycle of visions was coming to an end, I was asked to share what I had learned. But I soon discovered that I could not do it immediately. The impact of the experience generated a deep process of inner transformation that would last for many years to come.

During that time, I devoted myself to my family, the education of my children, and the cultivation of my inner life through reading, meditation, contemplation, and deep introspection. To better understand what had happened to me, I began to study dreams and mystical experiences through the lens of various psychological, spiritual, and religious traditions, in particular, Sufism with Llewellyn Vaughan-Lee. As I began to grasp the wisdom of the teachings I had received, they served as a lit candle, illuminating the steps of my path and helping me to embody a new understanding of being a woman. I became a holistic therapist and counselor and founded the Essential Oneness Feminine Wisdom Project. Soon after, I was asked by my former teacher, Llewellyn, to lecture on and teach meditation and dream analysis in South America and, eventually, to write my own autobiography,* where the subject of this book was briefly mentioned.

Now I feel the time is finally ripe to share my experiences and the teachings I received in my youth; for even though the feminine voice is gaining prominence in our society, her essence remains mostly in the shadows. That essence is part of a truth that patriarchal culture buried thousands of years ago and confined to the darkest corners of our memory. Yet its truth also remains in everything, and is within easy reach.

My intention has been to capture the essence of what I saw, heard, learned, and lived over a period of seven months

---

* *El Llamado de mi Corazon* was published in Spanish in 2014.

Prologue

more than twenty years ago now. It is a hard task, because the ways in which the feminine expresses herself are very different from that to which we are accustomed. Her message is circular, cyclical, spiraling. On each new turn she reveals, deepens, and expands a multi-leveled knowledge. Thus, her teachings are incorporated gradually, as they create an inner landscape that nurtures our soul and slowly fills life with purpose.

Parts I and II of this book describe my life before and around the time I arrived in the United States with my family, as well as my initial mystical experiences and visions. Parts III, IV, and V, narrate in a continuous manner the teachings I was given on the power of love and how it manifests. Part VI tells of the rebirth that takes place in us when we embrace the fundamental and sacred role of feminine wisdom in this critical moment of the world's evolution.

The visions described herein help us to understand the harm that patriarchy—by devaluing the feminine and her qualities—has caused women, men, and the Earth itself. They also carry valuable information needed to heal our wounds and help us build a very different world for future generations.

I trust that this vision can help you, as it did me, to remember the sacred nature of your feminine essence.

Part One:
Woman, Remember

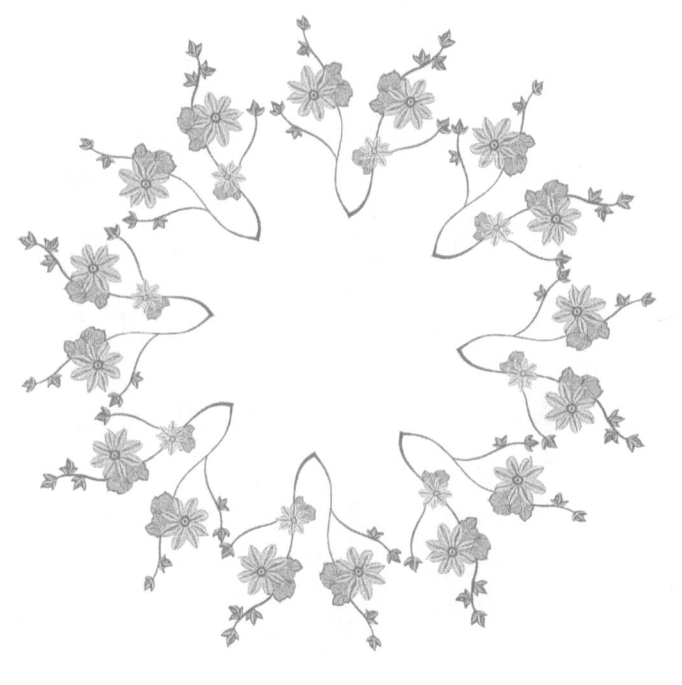

Chapter One
Beginnings

I was born in Cordoba, a state in the very heart of Argentina. Though destiny would take me away from my place of birth early, images of its sun-drenched landscape—fields of blossoming cosmos flowers, donkeys and guanacos grazing on the hillsides—have remained forever imprinted on my soul.

Traveling was almost a way of life for my family when I was a child, which may be why I have always been a bit of an adventurer. The many trips we took within the country and abroad—due to my father's work—are among the happiest of my childhood memories.

When I turned six, and it was time to start elementary school, we stopped accompanying my father when he traveled. My parents sought a more stable life for my younger brother and me and settled permanently in Buenos Aires. We moved to a neighborhood in the suburbs of the capital close to extended family and friends, and I enrolled in an all-girls Catholic school.

A dream at fourteen brought a considerable shift in my life; it was my first significant spiritual experience. In the dream, a man dressed in everyday clothes kissed me on the forehead; when he did so, we merged into each other until we became a single light, pure and blinding, and I was filled with absolute glory. When I came back to myself and could see my surroundings again, the man was now wearing a long white tunic and sandals and I knew he was a saintly being. The depth of the union I felt transformed my vision of reality; and from then on, I perceived everything—thoughts, actions, and events—as completely interrelated.

Remembrance

This unitive experience initiated my spiritual journey and sparked a keen interest in learning about the world religions and the fundamentals of philosophy and psychology. At the same time, the experience ignited a longing to explore the world with fresh eyes.

As soon as I finished high school, I went on my first trip abroad on my own, something quite unusual, and even discouraged, for young women from my country at the time. I flew to Spain and spent over two months wandering through Western Europe and England, absorbing the history, art, and cultural treasures of the places I visited.

One day, while walking on a street in Holland, an amazing school caught my attention. I looked through a classroom window and saw a meticulously designed space, with low furniture and beautiful rugs and paintings. Children of different ages came and went freely and calmly; they were reading, writing, preparing their snacks, and tidying up after themselves. The warmth of home had somehow been brought into the classroom in an organic, peaceful way. What I saw was so different from the classrooms I knew.

Later, when I was studying to become a teacher, the memory of that place led me to investigate alternative methods of education. I didn't quite know what I was looking for until I visited a school in Mexico that was similar to the Dutch one I had seen. I learned that the founder of the educational philosophy behind both schools was Dr. Maria Montessori, a groundbreaking scholar and educator, and Italy's first woman medical doctor.

I fell in love with the Montessori teachings and opened my own school inspired by this system as soon as I returned to Argentina. I was twenty-three years old. Some months later, I received a phone call from an eighty-year-old British woman named Frances, who had studied with Maria Montessori. Frances had heard of my school and offered to help, becoming my mentor and the school's godmother. The time I spent with her, the teachers, and students of my school filled me with joy. Day after day, for more than ten years, I devoted myself to

Beginnings

running it. I planned lessons, trained teachers, created didactic materials, and answered the many day-to-day demands that arose.

When I turned thirty-two, while studying in California, I met Walter, an American Montessori teacher who would become my life-companion. As our relationship became more committed, he decided to move to Argentina, and two years later we were married.

By then, the school had more than three-hundred students and forty teachers. Frances' wisdom and charisma had given it a special flavor, which helped me promote an educational method that was well-known in other countries but new to mine. It was in part due to this unfamiliarity that I often encountered resistance from certain parts of the community. I also faced opposition for being a young woman who had founded and was directing her own school. The new system and my roles clashed with the cultural values of the society in which I lived, which was accustomed to a more traditional way of teaching, and reluctant to let a young woman occupy a position of authority.

For a long time, I was able to deal with this friction, even finding in it a source of motivation. But toward the end of 1993, a group of people began to defame our work. My pain and stress became acute and there was little I could do to confront what was happening.

Around that time, another great change took place in my life: I became pregnant with twins. Four months earlier, a medical test had indicated that I could not bear children. So I received this unexpected announcement as a gift. My whole existence took on new meaning. My happiness increased with the passing of months, and the moment I saw my newborn babies, I felt a love for them that I had not known existed in me.

After this, Walter decided to pursue a career in law to better support our family, but his limited Spanish made this difficult. Thus, we moved to the United States.

Chapter Two
The Desert

We arrived in Charlottesville, Virginia, in the end of June 1996, and rented a townhouse walking distance from the University of Virginia School of Law, where Walter had recently been accepted. The summer months passed quickly: we spent some time at my in-laws in New York, traveled to surrounding towns, and visited nearby parks and beaches.

When classes started, Walter's studies took up almost all of his time; so I began to organize an independent routine for me and the children. I met a teacher from a Waldorf school and a homeopathic doctor, who introduced me to a group of mothers with young children that met weekly. We joined them. When the kids played, the mothers would talk—while preparing food or organizing crafts for the children.

The other days—when it wasn't raining—I would go with the twins to the nearby park, where they enjoyed the sandbox, slides, and swings.

Little by little, we established a routine.

By the end of November, when Christmas decorations began to adorn the streets, we were almost entirely adapted to our new country. Enthralled by the multicolored display of holiday ornaments, the twins asked me each day to take the path to the park through the open mall, which was full of these festive decorations. But it was during these last weeks of the year that I began to perceive the city as increasingly sad, opaque and lifeless, instead of the luminous and joyful place it appeared to be. Passing the local stores and restaurants was

Remembrance

like watching a movie where everything was made of plastic or cardboard, unreal and hollow.

I experienced this sensation again and again over a period of many days, and it made me uneasy. But, as I felt fine as soon as I walked through the front door of our home, I downplayed these feelings and adapted to them. I didn't know then that they were only a precursor to a shift in my consciousness.

One afternoon, as I crossed the street with my kids to enter the park, everything around me suddenly began to dissolve before my eyes—the sidewalk, the trees, the cars, the houses—shapes melting and colors fading, noises falling silent. Reality lost its firmness and sharp lines and became a discolored tide into which everything merged. The ground under my feet disappeared and I was completely suspended in emptiness. I lost my breath. Wherever I looked, I could see only a milky opaqueness. I felt as if I was dying.

Where were my children? I couldn't see them; but I felt their hands and held them tight against my body. I tried to call for help, but my voice was gone. A feeling of desperation overcame me, and an inarticulate cry began to rise up from the depths of my being. In that moment, I knew with certainty that if I were to die now, my life would have been lived in vain—wasted, because I had not *remembered*. It was the cry of my soul I was hearing. Up to that point, I had not felt as if my life was missing anything of significance, but now I was sure it was. There was something I had to remember, and I did not know what it was.

Slowly, the experience began to subside and my surroundings regained their varied colors and definite shapes. I felt my feet on the ground again, but my legs were shaking badly and my heart was pounding. My breath was agitated and I still couldn't find my voice. I wanted to cry, but I wouldn't allow it. It would have worried my kids. Instead, I pretended that nothing had happened and I simply walked with them up to the sandbox. We all sat down on the sand. While the children played, I tried to calm myself down.

The Desert

To say that I was bewildered would be an understatement. All my foundations had been demolished in an instant. *My life had been lived in vain? Mine?* I couldn't get over my astonishment. I had always felt that my life had meaning—as an educator, as a wife, and as mother. And yet I found myself receiving this incredible shock of knowing I had to *"remember"* something, without which, my entire life was wasted! But what was it?

Feeling profoundly alone, I sought out my old diary and began to pour into it everything that came into my mind—any and all ideas on what I needed to *"remember."* The exercise of writing drew me deeper and deeper into myself, taking me through the most arid inner desert I could possibly imagine.

Chapter Three
The Cloud

Several days after my death-experience in the park, I woke up with a fever. My body felt cold despite my temperature being quite high. Something told me that I needed to fast a few days; it was an internal order, precise and firm. Due to a bad experience with fasting in the past, the idea of fasting was not appealing; but in this case, I was thankful for a clear directive and didn't actually have a doubt about following it.

Walter made me a medical appointment. On the way to the doctor's office, we were delayed due to a traffic accident and arrived five minutes late. We missed our appointment and couldn't get another that day. So I returned home to rest. To avoid exposing our children to a possible infection, we decided that I would isolate myself in the master bedroom until the fever passed.

On the third day of fasting, while lying in bed, I noticed something hovering near the ceiling at the far side of the room, a kind of cloud. As I watched, it moved slowly along the ceiling toward me and stopped right above me. The Cloud was made of three rings. The outer ring was a dark pink, the middle green, and the center a twinkling star of liquid gold that palpitated like a beating heart. I didn't know what was happening, so I prayed to God for protection.

Time seemed to stop while an omnipresent silence permeated the bedroom. The Cloud moved down toward me and stopped right above my chest, at a distance of about three feet. From the golden heart of the Cloud extended an invisible tube, like an arm of emptiness, that touched the center of my chest and

Remembrance

reached into my heart. Through that "tube," I received a peace and love beyond description. At that moment, I understood the true meaning of "peace be with you." I had been given that peace. It was a greeting. My body relaxed completely and suddenly felt light as a feather, and I knew that I was in the presence of an angelic being.

In a split second, without words, I received several teachings that instantly shifted my understanding and perception of life, which would never return to the way it was before.

I understood that matter and spirit were one and the same, only differing in degree of density; that everything was *inside*, and that the *outside* did not exist; everything was One and the One was infinite. The other teachings I would only be able to put into words later.

My eyesight also changed: objects looked ethereal, as if made of energy which was more or less compact, like a weave, or like Swiss cheese, pierced by emptiness.

Peace and inner silence stayed with me after this encounter, and for many hours I remained in a profoundly introspective state, without words. Although I had had intuitions and psychic experiences previously, which had taught me that there was a reality beyond everyday reality, nothing I had previously experienced compared to this; nothing had been as deep and as intimate.

As I was getting ready to sleep that night, my body began to vibrate and grow warmer. The heat grew until an energetic center at the base of my spine opened. Strong vibrations emanated from this center and my back hurt. My head and the space above it began to shine and radiate light, and I saw a ray, similar to lightning, descend from the crown of my head to the base of my spine. When the ray reached my sacrum, the heat increased.

At some point, I fell into a half-sleep and had a brief dream which indicated that I should read a certain woman author (whose name my former teacher, Frances, had mentioned to me years before) so I that I would understand what was happening

The Cloud

to me. The following morning, Ana, my aunt and godmother in Argentina, called me. She told me that she missed the family and was coming to visit us in the summer. I asked her to bring me any books she could find by this author.

The experience of the previous day, and the continuing perception that my surroundings were ethereal, made me feel unrooted. It was hard to reconcile what my eyes were seeing with what my memory said I should be seeing. A pronounced level of psychic sensitivity had awakened in me.

I decided to end my fast. I thought eating would ground me and the new vibrations would diminish; I hoped I would feel more rooted and be able to assimilate what was occurring in my consciousness. But it would actually take a long time for that to happen; my body, heart, and mind had gone through a shock, whose depth I would only understand with the passing of years.

In the months that followed, I would feel waves of love, joy, heat, and cold, as well as an electric vibration circulating throughout my body, almost on a daily basis. When these waves diminished, I would be in a radiant paradise. I would become absorbed in it and observe my surroundings in silence. There were no thoughts. I enjoyed a deep state of being—peaceful and outside of time. I would connect with the outer world only to respond to the needs of my family and my home.

My kids played quietly near me, immersed in the stillness that surrounded us, no matter where we were. They didn't seem to mind my apparently absent state. But Walter, seeing how I had stopped being the multi-tasking woman he knew, was concerned.

When we went out or met friends, my silence mostly passed unnoticed. At home, however, I would come back *into myself*

Remembrance

to find Walter next to me, repeating my name or touching my arm, or with my kids pulling on my clothes, climbing onto my lap, or kissing my cheeks.

I consulted with a Jungian psychologist and an energetic therapist. Both of them assured me that there was nothing to fear. I was going through a psycho-spiritual process. This diagnosis seemed to quiet some of my husband's concerns.

Nevertheless, the nights were the biggest challenge. For almost a year, I could not sleep for more than two hours a day. Sometimes it was because of a brilliant light that seemed to emanate from within me, filling me with joy; but mostly it was because the currents of joy and energy increased in me throughout the day, starting slowly in the morning and becoming so intense by the evening that there was no way for my body to relax.

Occasionally, the internal vibrations were so powerful that Walter could feel them too, and was himself unable to sleep. He even slept in another room, temporarily. And yet I knew his worries stayed with me when he was sleeping, because I would see his energetic body return to check on me, wanting to make sure that I was okay, not really understanding what was happening to me.

In the late hours of the night, while everyone else slept, I would often leave my bedroom and go downstairs to the living room. There I paced, put things in order, and cleaned. This helped to relax me a little.

Chapter Four
The Ageless Woman

When the fever hit me, I stopped writing; but shortly after the apparition of the Cloud, I felt a need to write again.

The moment that I sat comfortably on my chair and placed paper on the table a potent diamond-light appeared above me. For a moment I could not see or hear anything; the luminosity and deep silence of that light permeated everything—a sweet fragrance of flowers, an audible prayer of praise to God, and a celestial music flooded me.

Then, somehow, a drop of this light entered through the top of my head and led me into another state of awareness, an infinite space. Even though I could feel my feet on the floor, and my body on the chair, I was somehow floating. And while floating, this light opened and poured its contents into me.

In an instant, I received the totality of a story that went to the core of my being and shook me like an earthquake. And yet, at the same time, that story seemed even less tangible than a gentle breeze. I grasped its content fully, but the message was so subtle that my mind could not begin to articulate it; it was too evanescent. It was a revelation about the nature of existence—the nature of life and creation, about its infinity, multidimensionality, interconnectivity, interdependence, parallelism—and of its patterns and timelessness within time. It left me with a taste of wonder, a sense that there was an intelligence and purpose beyond and within what manifested alternately as order or as chaos.

Remembrance

The following night I felt called to write again. I thought that writing might allow me to express what I had received the day before. It was 1:00 AM when I went downstairs to the living room. Outside it was raining and a freezing wind was blowing. The heater was on high, but did not do much to alleviate the cold. With fleece pajamas, thick socks and a shawl over my shoulders, my muscles were tense, trying to retain all the warmth they could. But as soon as I sat down, my consciousness shifted, my body relaxed, and I could no longer feel the cold. The space around me changed; it became soft and velvety. Again, I heard the prayers and music of the previous night and tiny drops of light that felt like gifts rained down on me.

I sensed presences, too. At first, I could not see them; I simply felt peace and love. Gradually, I began to see three beings floating in front of me. At no time did I feel any fear; I think the meeting with the Cloud had prepared me. They were transparent beings—*holy*. Once again, the perfume of flowers saturated the space.

My attention was directed toward one of these beings in particular, and I needed to close my eyes. As I did so, I had a slight sensation of dizziness, and I felt as if my mind were absorbed, taken to a new space, where I could see the semi-transparent image of a woman with long hair and a gentle face. Her eyes transmitted wisdom and goodness. In the beginning, she looked very old to me, but then I saw her young, and an instant later, she was older again. Her image changed continuously. She was an ageless woman. Suddenly, she felt familiar to me, as if I had known her from some time before. My thought processes and reactions slowed. I did not know what to do. Then she spoke to me with a soft firm voice:

"For some time I will come to you every day and be your guide on a journey. Write what you experience—the places you visit and what you learn and understand. I have much to show you and tell you. *Accompany me now.*"

Part Two:
The Journey

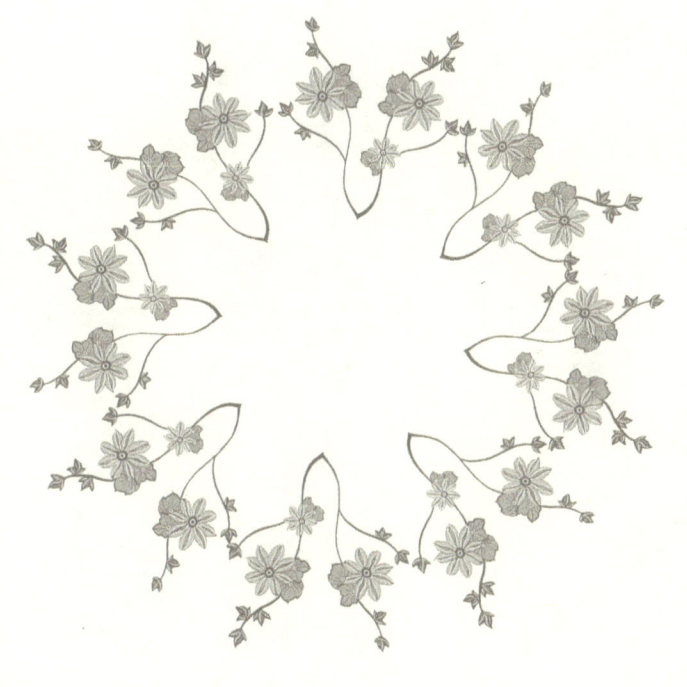

Chapter Five
A New Earth

A moment after the Ageless Woman spoke, I found myself in a resplendent place, amid uplifting music that was absolutely new to me. At first, I could not see anything but light. Little by little, I was able to make out my surroundings. I was on top of a hill with the Ageless Woman. We were standing on a sea of tall grasses and wildflowers that swayed in the breeze, the hum of bees joining the beautiful melody. The leaves of each plant, the air, and even the ground itself, seemed to be imbued by the music. It was a song of gratitude that began to seep into my body; I felt welcome and safe.

Below, on the hillside, I saw a lovely town—everything seemed so alive. The idea of *Heaven* crossed my mind. As if reading my thoughts, the Ageless Woman said, "This is not Heaven; it is the Earth."

Then, unexpectedly, my mind returned to this world, to my freezing room, the chair, the table, and the paper. Stunned, I looked at the clock; it was not yet three, and it was still raining. Less than two hours had passed. It had seemed much longer to me. I was dumbfounded, invaded by a torrent of feelings—bliss, doubt, hope, concern. I tried to keep calm, waiting for my emotions to quiet down.

Neither the Cloud nor the three transparent beings had caused me this much confusion. Those presences had revealed themselves in such a way that there was no room for doubt in me. But this new mix of vision and experience, this kind of lucid dream while awake, where I had felt transported to another place, was of a different nature. Part of me had been

Remembrance

taken to another dimension, and the prospect that this would continue daily caused me considerable apprehension.

I immediately wrote down what had occurred. I thought it would be easy: the experience had been so vivid that I could recall each detail of the place I had visited. But no matter how much I tried, I could not find the words to capture it fully. There was no way to describe the energy and the beauty I had encountered. The Earth I had visited was pristine, an Eden, where nature and the very air shone and sang. The phrase that came to my mind was "New Earth." I would later discover that this is indeed what it was.

When I returned there *in vision* the following day, it was dawn in New Earth. The Ageless Woman and I were on top of the hill again. The pure fresh air felt lighter and softer than the air I usually breathed. Mountains circled a broad valley almost in its entirety, and I could see a river meandering through it. The first rays of the sun tinted the snow of the highest peaks with the pink and yellow tones of sunrise.

We went down the hill toward the town. While walking, the rhythm of the music (always present) entered my body until it became so much a part of me that I could no longer discern where it came from.

"The music you hear and feel is the pulse of the Earth," said the Ageless Woman.

I wanted to ask her why she had brought me here, but I assumed that in time I would know.

The colors of the town were intense and vibrant, the houses charming. A plaza dotted with trees marked the heart of the place. There were sculptures, water fountains where birds bathed, benches where people conversed amiably, and many children playing.

A New Earth

Everything was very tidy and well maintained. The streets were bordered on both sides by tall deciduous trees, their branches full of buds, the sun's rays passing through them, warming us on our way. The tree trunks, thick and old, spoke of an urbanization from long ago; but somehow everything looked new. Instead of fences, lush gardens—displaying a mix of shrubs, vines, and fruit trees—separated one house from the other.

I could see signs of modern technology I had never seen before; but something in this place reminded me of country towns from my youth in Argentina that retained a particular flavor of the past—places where time passes slowly, and people exude tranquility and warmth. And there was something else: there was a perceptible joy, a certain lightness in peoples' steps, a seeming attention to every detail that amazed me.

People of different cultures and races walked by, tending to their chores, working, enjoying a moment of relaxation. I also noticed a certain dignity, a deep mutual respect, and a level of trust that bound it all together. There was a total absence of fear. I watched people giving thanks and blessings, even to animals and plants, the water and the air. I saw a welcoming ceremony for a newborn child.

In the New Earth, all people were appreciated and valued.

In my successive visits, the Ageless Woman took me to different areas of the town and its outskirts: historical sites, working and educational spaces, buildings of importance. I observed everything, and from time to time, I received a brief explanation.

The town was bordered on one side by the river, and on the other by two sectors vaguely defined: one for production with farms of a few acres each, and another for education and research. Farther out, there were fields and a totally wild preserve that reached the mountain range. The more I traveled, the more I noticed the balance between the natural and the human-made, and how through colors and materials, the buildings blended with the environment.

During my whole stay, I heard the music of the Earth. Although I kept mostly silent, observing and listening, with the passing days and visits, my presence there felt more and more real.

After each vision, I returned happy with the feeling of being in heaven. It seemed that I was learning how life *could be*. I tried to hear that lovely music in *this* reality; and yet, the experiences of that beautiful place brought me enormous doubts.

Where did this New Earth exist? I wanted to believe that it was a token, a proof of how the world could be; but was it? How could I know if everything I saw was not just an illusion or a fantasy? The delights and the peace I experienced with the Ageless Woman made me want more; but the fact that the visions came and went without my consent frightened me.

In the last vision of this period, the Ageless Woman and I took a path that crossed a poplar grove. We walked for a long while until we came to a stone arch—the entrance to a farm where sheep grazed in large green pastures. A slim, middle-aged woman with dark hair tied in a long braid, wearing a light-colored tunic reaching down to her ankles, was taking care of the flock. When she saw us, she came toward us with a friendly smile. While the subtle, almost transparent features of the Ageless Woman always eluded precise description, the shepherdess' features were well-defined.

The two women held hands and looked deeply at one another for a moment. Then the Shepherdess turned toward me and said, "Welcome." Just like the Ageless Woman, she did not introduce herself or ask me who I was.

We left the farm together and headed toward the river. Several times we passed people on the way who knew the Shepherdess and greeted her with a slight nod from a distance.

The fast waters of the mountain river, cold and completely clear, bathed a riverbank of large rocks, sand and pebbles. On the other bank, the river caressed the lowest branches of a variety of trees. Some women were sitting on the rocks nearby; the echo of their laughter reached us.

We stopped to rest on a beach covered by small stones with metallic flecks that glimmered under the sunlight. I was captivated. The idyllic life that I had read about in myths was here a reality. It was so simple, yet so beautiful and perfect. My eyes went from one sight to the next; I wanted to capture and keep that place in my memory forever.

Sometime later, the Shepherdess said she wanted to show me something and invited us to continue. We took a path that bordered the river, and then ascended a knoll. While going up, the Shepherdess looked at me and said, "Our people found the meaning of our life; and this led us to commit to a mission. We obtained our meaning in a special way. One day we decided to remember and never again to forget."

It was as if I had heard magic words. *Remember and never again to forget*. I was flooded by a sense of relief and breathed deeply. Since the moment I realized that my life would be wasted if I didn't remember, I had been searching for a sign of what I had forgotten. I had just received that sign.

We kept ascending the knoll, but I could no longer pay attention to the beautiful vista; my mind was immersed in the word *"remember."* Finally, I had met someone who might be able to help me find that forgotten purpose. I repeated internally, over and over, *"Remember and never again to forget."* That was what I wanted.

REMEMBRANCE

I returned to my everyday reality repeating these words. The happiness that I brought back this time had a different quality; it was charged with anticipation, with a sense of beginning.

The rest of that day, the fears that usually increased in me with the passing of the hours did not come. The wind of hope had blown them away, and I felt they would not return. I waited expectantly for the night to arrive and for the women of the New Earth to come and look for me.

Chapter Six
The Bearers of Remembrance

When I returned to the New Earth, the three of us—the Ageless Woman, the Shepherdess, and I—were standing before two tall columns that marked the entrance to an amphitheater, a large platform circled by stone steps, which was built into the natural slope of the hill. We walked up to the center of the arena where a golden plaque was anchored to the floor.

"This is the Place of Remembrance," said the Shepherdess, pointing at the words engraved on the metal plaque. The natural acoustics of the amphitheater amplified and created an echo from her words.

"Here, the past and present interweave to generate and bring meaning to our 'today' and our 'tomorrow.' Here, we remember ourselves, who we are, what we came to do. Here, in this very place, are told the feats of our ancestors, feats that guide each of us in our present day.

"A legend says that in order to remember, our ancestors decided to investigate the history of their peoples, cultures, and traditions, as far as they could reach into the past. They stamped all the facts they discovered onto large pieces of white linen cloth. Then they did the same with the history of the planet and the universe, and decided not to hide information from one another, or distort the truth, no matter how difficult or painful.

"When they knew their history and the paths they had walked, they realized that they had made great mistakes, and that some of those mistakes had almost led them to destroy

Remembrance

themselves and the planet. So they wept for a long time, and repented.

"After a long period of contrition, each of our ancestors asked forgiveness, and they were forgiven, and forgave themselves. Forgiveness was found in the valuing of all their experiences, both positive and negative, as parts of a necessary learning process. They chose to unite all the knowledge they had acquired with what they called 'The Golden Thread of Existence,' sewing together and arranging all the pieces of this white linen, which was stamped with all the common details or characteristics of their stories.

"Soon, our ancestors realized that they could continue combining those groupings of information in new ways, and they began to unite the pieces of cloth into larger and larger units.

"It was then that they noticed that the borders of the pieces of linen cloth—those separate pieces of material sewn with the gold thread—began to dissolve into unity, until one could not really tell they had ever been separate. Thus, all the pieces eventually became one single piece of fabric. But this greater cloth was not white like the original pieces of linen. It had transformed into a beautiful, delicate, translucent material, comprised of all the colors of life, saturated by the golden flow of the gold thread.

"Without their knowledge, they had discovered the formula to dematerialize matter.

"With this new fabric, they made a magnificent garment that radiated golden light, and they called it, 'The Suit' or 'Garment of Remembrance.'"

While the Shepherdess was speaking, the Ageless Woman lifted her arm and made a circular movement with her hand. At that moment, a golden light illuminated the whole arena, and I saw the exquisite Garment of Remembrance floating in the air.

"This garment belongs to all of us; and though no one wears it, all of us know that part of our story exists in it. We know that our actions will remain stamped onto the fibers of its

The Bearers of Remembrance

cloth, so that we may remember our connection with everyone and everything, and not forget the function we have come to perform. Our ancestors discovered their siblinghood with all of the beings of the Earth. They knew, as human beings, that they were the eyes and ears of the planet, the awakened consciousness of creation on Earth, and that their mission was to love, care for, and protect the world and its beings."

As she was speaking, I could not take my eyes off the garment. I felt the strand of my own life interwoven in its fabric.

"One day, while looking at the garment, our ancestors realized that the radiant translucence of the cloth might be a clue, a secret they needed to uncover. Following this clue, they discovered their own true essence. They were like the Garment of Remembrance: transparent and radiant beings with a physical form. They were a spark of spirit made flesh. They understood that this was also true of the Earth: she, too, was a being of light with a physical body.

"Their discovery led them to uncover more and more mysteries, until they recognized their connection with the invisible universe, and indeed, with all the universes. They realized that they were themselves the intersection between the physical and celestial worlds; and they knew themselves to be one with everyone and *all*, made of the same essence.

"Since then, we not only care for the planet and all its beings, whom we consider as the love of the divine embodied as matter, but we also bear witness to the spirit of life in the universe, which we call 'the breath of divinity that animates all things.'

"This is the reason why our ancestors began to call themselves 'Bearers of Remembrance.' They had remembered who they were, where they came from, and where they were going. They were a creation of the single source.

"Generation after generation, we relive this remembrance within our own hearts and reach this same realization, so that for each one of us, the reality of our oneness with *all* becomes a daily, living experience. Life is a gift that gives us a unique opportunity to learn, develop and perfect an aspect of ourselves. We call this learning an experience of the material, the experience of being souls, living a physical existence.

"The Earth is the paradise we were given to care for and preserve in this corporeal experience. That is why harmonizing with her is our law."

The Ageless woman added:

"The vocation of the bearers of remembrance is to bear witness to and affirm the presence of the sacred in the world. Their job is to bring awareness to a living universe that does not know itself. It is to contemplate the sunrise for a sun that does not know it dawns, to admire the grandeur of the mountain for a mountain that does not know its majesty, to appreciate the perfume of the flower for the flower that does not know its own perfume. It is to gratefully experience the paradise of the Earth for an Earth that does not know she is a paradise."

Slowly the image of the Garment of Remembrance faded from sight and we left the Place of Remembrance and walked back on the path that had taken us there. I pondered the legend as we walked. The idea that the humanity of the New Earth could be our future, and the world I lived in could one day be like this one, filled me with optimism; but I dared not ask if this would be so.

As soon as my mind returned to this reality, I wrote the 'legend' down. My first interpretation was that the legend was a story about the end of the world, though quite different from how I had learned it in my Christian upbringing and education. It alluded to mistakes and repentance, of course, but also to a consciousness of integration, to the possibility of discovering a meaning in life and a commitment to it.

The Bearers of Remembrance

During this vision, I hoped that the New Earth and its people would be the future of our world; now it occurred to me that it might just be an allegory for my own life, and of a process that could help me to remember. I decided to ask if this were true.

Chapter Seven
The Time of the Descent

When I arrived, the two women were waiting for me. We were in a large field on a cool afternoon. There were birds, a few clouds in the sky, and in the distance, a group of goats were coming down the mountainside. The breeze carried the voices of singing children from somewhere nearby.

"Is this the Earth of the future? . . . Is this my future?" I wanted to know.

"It is the future . . . and it is also a possibility," responded the Ageless Woman.

"The story she"—the Shepherdess—"told you indicates that much suffering was required to achieve the necessary understanding to reach this place. In a person, it can take years, even a lifetime. For the life of the Earth, it would take millennia."

The Shepherdess added: "It took years upon years of pain, grief, and incomprehension. It required reflection, effort, and much help to come out of this long period of pain. Within the fibers of the Garment of Remembrance, these events remain, imprinted, and we remember and learn from what happened in those days."

"I want this Earth to be possible," I said. "I want to remember and never again to forget. I want to know the forgotten part of the meaning of my life and to live it."

"The meaning of one's life is one's own," the Ageless Woman continued, "but invisible threads weave it into the meaning of the life of the rest of humanity, and of the Earth.

Remembrance

What is done for oneself is done for all; the meaning of life is something that is found in oneself, and also at the heart of humanity. The meaning of one's life is neither a concept nor a belief or a technique; it does not come from outside, but from inside. There are ways to find it and to live it."

"Where should I start?" I asked.

"At the moment," the Ageless Woman said, "by seeing what happened in the world, and in your own world; because your small world exists within a larger one. What happens to one, directly or indirectly, happens to all."

After a pause, the Ageless Woman said seriously, "It is time."

She pointed to the sky, moved her arm in a circle, and the Garment of Remembrance reappeared, floating. One of its golden threads extended from it and became longer and longer, until it formed a square. Within the square, as if it were the frame for a work of art, I saw the Earth, luminous, with blue, green, and brown areas, turning in space. On one of the frame's corners, dark storm clouds emerged. They moved toward the world, surrounded it, and covered it, until the Earth disappeared behind a gray layer, pierced by red rays of light.

"The Earth," said the Shepherdess, "has gone through periods of light and periods without light. In our annals, each of these periods received a particular name. The most difficult period was known as 'the *Descent.*' "

As she said this, the image vanished, leaving the frame empty.

Silence.

Then, within the frame, began a thunderous bombardment of terrible scenes that showed the bleakest events of that long period called "the Descent." The images were like slides, one after another, bombarding me with sight, sound, and smell . . .

The Time of the Descent

People wrapped in dirty rags,
    fighting for pieces of moldy bread.
Some so emaciated they could barely walk.
Others, ill, fell and died in the middle of the street.
An odor of disease and death pervaded.
People walked among the dead,
    indifferent to them.
Someone stole from an ailing person.
Collapsed roofs, holes in walls.
Barricades of rubble.
Families seeking places to hide,
    running through the streets,
    jumping over streams of fetid water
    and pools of fresh blood.
Soldiers fought civilians;
    armed civilians attacked the unarmed.
Large machine guns firing.
All of a sudden,
    a man exploded like a bomb.
Shots fired in the dark,
    followed by moans of pain, screams.
People shouted the name of God.
Killing, hunting, torture of defenseless people.
Desperate cries and the smell of burning.
War engulfed towns, villages, cities,
    then spread through the seas and into the air.

Remembrance

The ground shook and split in two.
Waters trembled and enormous waves destroyed towns,
    drowned people and animals alike.
Torrential rains flooded rivers and cities.

In some places, there was heavy snow,
    others drought.
A scorching sun burned woods and crops.
The Earth vacillated—freezing, boiling—
    jungles became deserts, glaciers melted.
Vast swaths of felled trees in the millions.
Mountains of refuse.
Oceans full of black oil, islands of garbage.
Dead fish.
Dark smoke rising from burning trash,
    a putrid steam emanating from their depths.
People coughing.
Others walking on rubbish, scavenging,
    living in makeshift huts with walls
    and roofs of garbage.
Cartloads of uneaten food, fresh,
    but thrown into trashcans and
    transported to the mountains of refuse.
Yet, also, piles of golden coins,
    brilliant gems, and metals.
Broken windows and doors.

The Time of the Descent

Everywhere rampant robbery.
Rats, cats, and wild dogs fought with people over food.
People enclosed by walls of showcases,
    looking and buying,
    throwing away and buying more.

Others bought and bought,
    but threw nothing away.
Rooms overflowed with paper, plastic,
    and stacks of boxes.
Everything was for sale—
    land, people, the Earth, all for sale.
People walked, worked, and ate in a hurry,
    giving each other sideways glances of distrust.
Families lived under black clouds,
    amid moonless and starless nights,
    amid sunless days,
    everything grey.
Many worked day and night;
    slept at work, lived at work.
Factories closed.
People wandered, knocked at doors,
    pleading to no avail.
Others yelled and protested.
Others covered their eyes and ears.
Others looked at papers they could not read
    and signed them.

Remembrance

Empty homes among the fields and trees.
Masses swarmed to soot-blackened cities.
Violence against those who looked different.
Violence against women.
Violence against children.
Violence against animals.
Elders ejected from their homes.
Many vagabonds, indigent and homeless.
Broken bottles, syringes,
   pills and powders, strewn on the ground
   where people slept, laughed, and cried alone.

I returned to my world with the echo of cries reverberating in my ears, my chest burning. I was breathless and bathed in tears. Chills ran through my body. The pain I felt was like a needle, the hope of the previous day became anguish.

The images, full of cruelty, came in waves and flooded my mind, again and again, drowning me in sorrow, reminding me that I had witnessed what I was just shown in various ways throughout my life. Although I had always felt grief and frustration for these situations, I now saw that a part of me, without realizing it, had accepted them as merely *'the way things are.'*

That part of me waited for an external salvation; while another part, in order to avoid suffering, looked elsewhere, in search of a different life, intending to save those I loved and myself, keeping us removed from the unkindness of the world.

When confronted with this montage of horror, I knew I had witnessed a hell of human invention, a hell in which there was still much to endure. The vision had confirmed it. I felt guilty, small, and impotent, and was silent for the rest of the day.

The Time of the Descent

At night, when the Shepherdess called, I trembled. I feared what was to come, but said nothing. The three of us—the Shepherdess, the Ageless Woman, and myself—were at the same place as the past vision. It was still cold, and there was some wind, but no clouds. We walked to a small meadow and sat among chamomile flowers.

The Shepherdess spoke softly now. In the future, she said, she would explain to me the vision in detail, the meaning of that part of history, and how the world had overcome that period.

"The story of 'the Descent' is the story of a cycle of light that darkened. Each cycle has its own characteristics, colors, and forms, a special quality that initiates them and, in a way, defines them. That cycle began as an opportunity of great advancement; but in the course of this period, something happened, and its energy of progress became toxic."

"I am part of that story," I said, heartbroken. "The Descent is the time that my world lives in now, isn't it? How can we reach this other Earth?"

The Ageless Woman answered, "To reach this Earth from your time, it is necessary to remember. Remembering implies unlearning what was learned, and beginning to look at life with other eyes. To look at life with other eyes, one needs to listen to the story of life offered with a new voice—the wise and feminine voice of love, soul, and body of existence. Each person that walks the path of love brings this possibile Earth closer."

I then returned to this world, filled with questions I had not had time to ask. I felt impatient over having to wait for the moment when the meaning of these times, and how to transcend them, would be explained to me. I was anxious

Remembrance

because I did not know how long it would take me to travel the path ahead of me.

I felt sorry for myself over my destiny. I made a list of all of my longings and frustrations, and the reasons why it was imperative to have answers at that very moment. Slowly, the affliction subsided, and the complaints were left behind. I was able to see how much hope and promise there were in the words of the Ageless Woman and the Shepherdess. I understood that I needed to wait.

Part Three:
The Passages

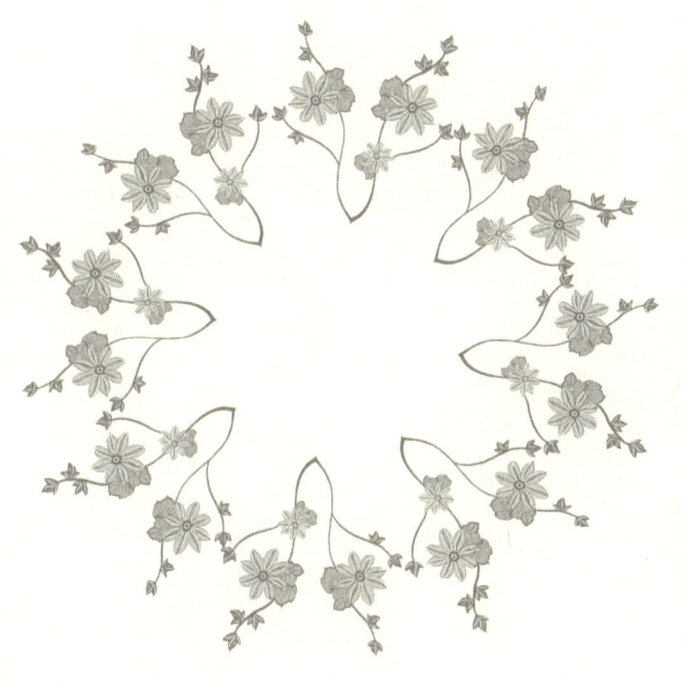

THE FIRST PASSAGE:
Creation

"Physical beings carry, at the core of their structure, a map of return to their essential nature, a subtle memory of their belonging to something beyond themselves, beyond their physicality."

— The Ageless Woman

Chapter Eight
The Mother

A new cycle of visions began the following day. Each night, for a period of several months, I felt my consciousness transported to the New Earth, and other dimensions, where I received teachings on the nature of love—the feminine face of the divine.

I travelled through different planes of existence, and from each one I returned with a new teaching that was connected to the prior one, and which expanded my understanding and knowledge of the great web of life.

The Ageless Woman and the Shepherdess were my guides on this path of feminine wisdom.

When I next returned to the New Earth, the Ageless Woman was at the pebble beach, where we had been before. It surprised me that the Shepherdess was not there. The Ageless Woman noted this and said that just the two of us would be traveling for a while.

It was a sunny afternoon. The river ran fast, and fed by the melting ice, seemed deeper than at other times. We left the beach and walked toward one of the snow-capped mountains. The forested hillside had tall and thin young pines, interspersed with older conifers with thick trunks. Even with no path in sight, the Ageless Woman knew the way.

Remembrance

We ascended for a long time. The woods grew thicker, and the rocky terrain became dusted with snow and harder to climb. It got dark, and I began to worry that the night might find us in this place. But then we passed a clearing, and I could see the sky. To my surprise, the sun was still high and dusk a few hours off.

We proceeded a little farther until, finally, the Ageless Woman stopped.

"Look," she said, pointing at an area of the woods. At first, I only saw more conifers and patches of snow; but then I noticed a pathway that opened between two large jutting rocks. As we began to walk in that direction, the path disappeared. A moment later, I saw it again; but then it vanished even as I was looking at it.

"It is a passage," said the Ageless Woman mysteriously.

Seeing that "passage" filled me with curiosity, and anxiety. As we came closer, I began to hear music, and I recognized it immediately. Tears filled my eyes. "Angels," I said to myself and quickened my step.

Once I crossed that mysterious threshold, I entered another world, and a different state of consciousness. The space was pure energy, golden light, and infused with that melody, commingled with the voices of a choir. I filled my lungs with the music and the prayers I was hearing. Just as before, I perceived a familiar aroma of flowers and sensed a presence, then another, and then one more. A loving peace came over me, and I knew that it came from these angelical beings. I closed my eyes and kept still, just feeling and enjoying that peace.

The Ageless Woman placed the palm of her hand over my closed eyes. When she removed it, I opened my eyes and saw with a much clearer vision and was able to make out my surroundings. I saw three transparent beings that shone from within, similar to the Cloud. They were larger than me and floated; each one had a different degree of transparency and radiated light of a different hue. Somehow, I knew that

The Mother

the different colors and degrees of transparency expressed a specifically beneficial quality; though all three emanated love and peace.

I was overcome with shyness, despite my great joy. With a simple gesture, the Ageless Woman introduced me to the angelic beings, and an exchange without words began. They infused me with their message. I was so fascinated that no questions came to my mind—I just absorbed what they were transmitting.

They said that, although they were invisible to the human eye, under certain circumstances, humans could smell their fragrance; and if it was the divine will, they could make themselves visible, most often to children. They live outside of time as we know it, in the continual present, and are eternal in comparison to us.

They told me that they do not belong to the Earth, and yet are present here in a particular way: the angelic universe, which some call "heaven," is interwoven with our physical universe. Each class of angels has a specific mission and function; certain groups are more related to human beings than others, and dwell among them. The "protectors" are the closest to humanity, being the angels that can most easily communicate with us.

Now the feeling of peace increased; it almost seemed to have weight. Everything was still and blissful; there was a fragrance of innocence, like the smell of a newborn child. I was delighted; I could have stayed there forever.

All at once, I was in a vast space, which seemed infinite. It was so immense that my mind stretched to its limits trying to grasp it. I tried to open myself to the infinitude, and may have received some help, because I was inexplicably able to stay there. The music was louder here, the peace deeper, and the love more embracing.

The light became subtler, and was permeated with soft rainbow hues. A freedom I had never known dissolved me. Before me, there was a celestial being utterly different from

Remembrance

the three I had just met. Its body, just like the environment, was almost invisible, with only the smallest hint of an outline. She radiated a nearly blinding light, and a double current of sparking energy poured from her core. This double current then split into two torrents, which advanced and receded like waves, expanding throughout the space, surrounding and enveloping her, so that I could never see her fully. I knew that unlike the other three beings, this one had several holy qualities and served as a guide to others.

Then, suddenly, I found myself back in the woods, on the other side of the passage, with the Ageless Woman. I had no idea how long we had spent in the angelic world. It seemed only a few minutes; but a heavy layer of snow now covered everything, which suggested that a long time had passed.

We started back slowly. A soft light marked our path. As we descended, I realized that it was now early morning.

The encounter with the angelic beings had left me in an altered state of consciousness.

While descending the mountain, I said, "I have never seen anything like that last angel before."

The Ageless Woman nodded and instructed me:

"The double current of energy you saw emanating from that great being is the energy of the power of love, the mightiest force in the universe, which emanates from the source. It is an energy that has often been misunderstood. When it reached the world, it split into two—*pure love* and *pure power*.

"Since then, both energies have been seeking to reunite, to become one again—the power of love. Pure love and pure power are twin forces, both living in all things. Pure love is a force of cohesion that unites and attracts. Pure power expresses as an impulse, a push that can initiate, separate, or end something.

"Each generation attempts to understand these forces. They have been called by many names, and many stories, songs, and poems, have been told, sung, and recited about them. They were seen in thousands of forms, from gods to demons, from

The Mother

ferocious animals to docile creatures. They were adored and feared; it was even forgotten that they were energies. They were seen as opposites. Pure power became masculine and pure love, feminine. Thus, they were further separated, and it became more difficult to reunite them.

"Human beings have the intrinsic capacity to balance and reunite pure love and pure power in themselves, to make them work together again. But time has distanced these forces to the degree that their union rarely occurs. They are almost always out of balance, and one usually prevails over the other, or only one of them develops while the other remains dormant.

"Creation is an embodiment of the power of love. This is true in the physical as well as the angelic realms. But, unlike the human realm, where the forces are out of balance, in the celestial realm, pure love and pure power manifest in their original form."

The Ageless Woman paused in her explanation, and we kept walking in the direction of the river. We arrived at the beach when the sun had just disappeared behind the mountains, and the sky was slowly darkening. There was no one there. Neither the lights nor the noises of the town reached us. The sound of the running water captured all of my attention. Then the Agelesss Woman resumed her explanation:

"The energy of the power of love existed before the physical universe, and even before the universe of the angels. The power of love is infinite love in action.

"Of the birth of this love and its mission, little is known. What is known can only be transmitted in allegory. It is the first birth of creation.

"In the beginning of the beginning, there was only the source, a single essence, eternal, infinite, and omniscient; it lived alone in its own existence, and had in itself all possibilities.

"One day, the source wished to see itself and could not. For that, one needs a mirror. So, its nature began to divide internally into two aspects—*created* and *uncreated*—while still remaining whole. The uncreated became the desire to see itself, and the created became a mirror. This mirror was made of a very subtle energy that emanated from the source as its desire arose, and became a fiber that wove itself into a thread.

"That fiber was the power of love, a primordial energy charged with wisdom, capable of nesting the spirit of life.

"When the source looked at itself in the mirror, what it saw reflected was its love, a love as infinite, wise, and powerful as itself. Thus, the mirror and its reflection were the first creation: a first layer of the created.

"This first creation was like a mantle, an eternal layer, completely pure and original, thinner, more ethereal and invisible than everything, and yet, the strongest of all, capable of holding and enclosing all the universes, and all creation. For this reason, the power of love became the Mother of Creation: the womb of infinite and unconditional love that contains everything, embraces everything, and accepts everything.

"Every so often, the uncreated wished to see itself in a new way, and each time the Mother of Creation conceived a new layer, made with the threads of her own being, the fiber of existence—all of them manifestations of love, all of them capable of containing the spirit of life.

"All these layers would become known as mothers whose wombs homed universes, worlds, and more."

I looked at the sky now. It was deep and vast. The Cosmic Mother was limitless—pearls and diamonds, the moon and the stars adorned her infinite body. I kept still for a long time, absorbed in the beauty of the night.

Chapter Nine
The Universe

When I returned from my reverie, the sun was just rising, the firmament an intense pink. I heard the sound of roosters somewhere nearby and saw the Ageless Woman sitting next to the river. As I approached, I noticed that where she was seated, the river formed a small pool of calm water that reflected our figures in the smallest detail.

The water looked fresh, and I was thirsty, so I cupped some with my hands, trying not to disturb our image. I drank and sat down, listening to the sounds of the valley and the town slowly awakening.

"Just as this water reflects us, creation reflects the uncreated," said the Ageless Woman, who in that moment looked very old, although her eyes held a youthful vivacity. Her white hair seemed soft, almost like foam.

"Among the many stories of the creation of the physical universe," she said, "there is one that tells of the help the angels provided to the mother of creation.

"When the mother of creation wanted to bring into existence a physical layer, a universe that would reflect infinite love, and nest the spirit of life in matter, she could not create something so concrete herself. Her fibers were too subtle. So to fulfill her mission, she sought the help of the angels, whose universe already existed and already possessed some density.

"Angels have always been the devoted servants of the One, so they immediately agreed to assist in any way they could. They knew that their universe had come into existence through the energy of the power of love, due to a wish from the

49

uncreated. They also knew substance, because their universe had been created out of a very delicate matter, almost non-existent from the physical point of view. This gave them the capacity to imagine a still denser dimension that did not yet exist."

As the Ageless Woman spoke, we were surrounded by a kaleidoscope of butterflies. Two rested on my shoulder, flapping their wings slowly. When the Ageless Woman saw them, she smiled, and her appearance was rejuvenated. Her long hair became blond, and swayed as if fluttering in the wind. With a graceful movement, she stood up, unfolded her arms, and began to turn softly in a slow dance, her entire being youthful.

Sitting by her side sometimes made me forget that she was not a woman of flesh and blood. I did not know if she was an angel, an archetype, a deity, a representation of the goddess, a saint, or a symbol of the ancestral feminine essence. What I did know is that she was not entirely physical. She belonged in the invisible world.

The changes in her appearance transmitted a message to me: in the young woman, I saw adventure, strength, a desire to move forward and love passionately. In the old woman, I found wisdom, peace, respite, accomplishment, and the love that makes understanding, as well as the capacity to look back and grasp meaning.

While I was thinking about this, the Ageless Woman stopped turning and became old again. She sat down next to me and continued:

"The softness of butterflies—the joy and mystery they awaken around them—reminds me of angels. Butterflies experience the oneness of life and dance that oneness as they visit each flower. When their caterpillar bodies grow wings and are free to fly, they experience the mystery of total transformation, and of life in two different worlds.

"Like them, the angels were aware of the existence of more than one universe. They knew their universe, the universe of

The Universe

the mother of creation, and the universe of the uncreated. They realized that, in order to help create a material universe, they needed the participation of all three universes.

"The angels began their work by conceiving a point-nexus with all the power of love they were able to transmit. They imagined it to be made from the essence of their own substance, a quality of light and love within them, that they were capable of increasing in themselves.

"Once their conception of this nexus was complete, the angels placed it at the confluence of their universe and universes of the mother of creation and the uncreated, so that they too could infuse it with their gifts and blessings.

"The gift and blessing of the uncreated reached the conception of the nexus, and as this was happening, the mother of creation bound them tightly with invisible threads of her own fiber, which contained her own gift and blessing.

"The intention of these celestial beings was successful, and the conception of this tiny nexus, this granule of the future material cosmos, became a reality. The newborn nexus, having incorporated the possibility of developing a denser body as a means of existence, also received the wisdom of infinite love and the secret of being from the mother of creation, as well as the infinite possibilities and secret of nonbeing from the uncreated, and the loving radiance of the angelic realm, too. All physical beings carry all these gifts inside them. At the core of their structure, there is a map allowing them to return to their essential nature, a subtle remembrance of their belonging to something beyond themselves, beyond their physical being.

"The nexus became so brilliant that it illuminated all, and began to slide out of the angelic world. The nexus created an infinitesimal 'place' for itself, which contained it and expanded, accommodating its need for growth. This expansion, or accommodation, was similar to rolling, a movement that would later become known as 'primordial time.'

"It was primordial time that allowed the nexus to begin to incarnate and densify. But its embodiment was so subtle that

Remembrance

it seemed non-existent from the perspective of the physical universe. For the angelic beings, however, the point-nexus was magnificent, beautiful, radiant, having acquired more potency than even they had imagined.

"The radiance of the nexus increased and gained such colossal power that it became uncontainable, burst and birthed. Myriad particles of the point-nexus dispersed and spread, pushed by the force of the explosion. The particles rolled back and reunited until they formed a single nexus again. A wrapping formed over the new point-nexus, covering and transforming it into a 'seed' with a radiant nucleus from the celestial world and a body of light from the physical world.

"This was the first embodiment of the power of love.

"The newly-born seed gained strength and power until it also became uncontainable. It exploded into an uncountable number of particles that dispersed and spread again, occupying more and more space, expanding the new physical universe.

"What had taken place with the original point-nexus repeated with the physical seed of light and there were many successive explosions."

As the Ageless Woman spoke, her story came to life and brilliant images of what she described appeared all around me. It was as if I were standing in the midst of the beginning of creation, as she said:

"Again, groups of particles formed and, as they continued rolling, densified and reunited, becoming larger formations. Many of these clusters also exploded and dispersed, and many of their particles combined, some absorbed others or disappeared. The larger formations became celestial bodies that continued moving and expanding the limits of space, forming 'families.'

"This process of birthing, union, separation, and transformation, will continue for as long as the life of the material cosmos continues.

The Universe

"Thus, the power of love incarnated as the material universe; its unifying force became the energy that binds it together. The new universe would come to be known as the 'cosmic mother,' and her womb, 'outer space.'

"The angels were completely engrossed with the beauty and radiance of creation. They perceived the luminosity that all particles carried within themselves. The creation of the universe was the most amazing spectacle the celestial world had ever witnessed—a pure and potent act of love, a 'miracle.'

"Many wished to participate in the further development of those stellar bodies, and their request—the secret longing of the Uncreated—was immediately granted.

"Their *'participation'* would be a service and offering to the physical universe, their *'role'* to protect and guide stars and planets. The work of the angelic beings would follow the divine plan to construct a bridge between realms, so that one day the material universe would recognize its true nature.

"Like a gust of wind, those great beings reached the spheres and became one with them. A ray of bliss blessed their unions. Filled with the love of the angels, the celestial orbits became a dance of gratitude."

The beauty of the story amazed me, but I wondered how I was to understand it in relation to what I already knew. As we left the beach, I asked the Ageless Woman, "Is this a metaphor?"

The Ageless Woman responded: "The version of the story that you know of the 'origin of life' is not the whole story. There is another account that complements and gives it a new meaning. It is the story of the creation of the mother. Since this story belongs to a dimension beyond time and space, it needs both metaphor and the language of your world's scientific discoveries."

Chapter Ten
Being

The Ageless Woman and I spent the days that followed visiting the surroundings of the town. We were mostly in silence, simply admiring the view. The weather continued getting warmer; the trees grew new light green leaves; the fields bloomed, and the bellowing and bleating of newborn calves and lambs accompanied us everywhere we went.

"It is the creative capacity of life that gave birth to everything that exists in the physical universe. This miracle was the reason why the angels wished to protect it," said the Ageless Woman one afternoon, as we strolled in a park. She paused for a while and then continued:

"Among the many celestial bodies that inhabited the concrete universe, there was one in particular that attracted the attention of the angelic realm. It was a small planet guided by a great angel. This planet was 'Earth.' There, the power of love had been pulsing so strongly that the Earth desired to bring a new expression of life into existence. Creating a new level of existence was such delicate work that it required the active participation of the protecting angel of the planet during the entire process."

At that moment, a great light shone over us, and a soft, clear and potent voice said, "Like all things in the universe, Earth has a soul. Earth is filled with the spirit of life, and with a deep motherly love. Her heart is pure. Earth and I are one. In the beginning, I embraced her, and we merged into one another."

I knew it was the protecting angel of the planet that spoke, and was about to ask her name when the Ageless Woman explained to me:

Remembrance

"Non-angelic beings cannot know the true names of angels. This is why humans have always called them by their primary attributes and functions. The qualities of this angel are purity, light, and love."

Then, the angel's luminosity entered my chest, touched my heart, and disappeared, leaving behind a mantle of quietude.

Sometime later, the Ageless Woman came to me and whispered in my ear, "Listen now—the voice of the Earth."

She had not even finished saying these words when I found myself in the calm of the eye of a hurricane with a gale encircling me. From this place, I heard the whistling of the wind, the clapping of thunder, the crashing of waves, the hissing of flames, the whoosh of rushing water, the crackling of embers, the rumbling of tremors, the tapping of rain, followed by the most *resounding silence*. Earth spoke in the most ancient of tongues, and my heart understood.

The experience was so intense that I lost awareness of where I was at that moment.

Evening had fallen, and the birds were already flying to their nests. In the distance, the glow of the lights of the town could be seen. We headed in that direction. As we walked, the Ageless Woman said:

"From the time of her creation, the Earth wanted to conceive a body capable of containing the soul of a being with the capacity to create, one that could appreciate and protect its surroundings—an independent being, with free will, who would come to know all the wisdom of love. Earth is a physical layer, a manifestation of infinite love and its wisdom that embodies the spirit of life. The gestation of her desired creation would take a long time. It would be a conception governed by the rhythms of matter.

Being

"In the beginning, the wisdom of love was asleep in the dense matter of the Earth. But, little-by-little, it began to awaken, wanting to free itself from its dense physical limitations so that it could express itself.

"As it freed itself, slowly, wisdom would begin to manifest as a natural intelligence that would express itself in different ways. It would take the form of sensation, emotion, memory, feeling, and cognition, until they became self-aware. Then it would begin to reveal itself as reflection and comprehension.

"Having reached that point, the conditions for the arrival of the being for which the Earth had long wished would be complete.

"For the angelic world, the fulfillment of Earth's desire was also of great importance, because that being would become a conscious bridge between the worlds.

"Angels lack autonomy. They are like the rays of the sun; they are emanations from the divine source. They are united to the source, and know neither independence nor choice, unlike the being that would soon come.

"Instead, angels know something the being of the Earth would ignore and would have to discover on its own—that its core is a spark of light, a soul, that is also a divine emanation."

The Second Passage:
Transformation

"Through the different forms of life on Earth, an ever vaster and more encompassing love was embodied, until it achieved the human being, who has the capacity to love infinitely, and to know they love infinitely."

— The Ageless Woman

Chapter Eleven
The Waters of Life

A few days later, the Ageless Woman and I left the town and went to the south end of the valley. We passed large sown fields and stepped upon a trail. The vegetation became increasingly scarce as we walked. Behind some bushes along the path, I saw a kind of reflection. I thought it could be a mirror, or a glass, that reflected the plants, but it vanished before I could tell what it was. A second later, it reappeared and I knew it was another passage.

This time, I could not imagine what might be on the other side; unlike the previous passage, no sound came from its depths. Thorny branches covered it almost completely. I followed the Ageless Woman up to its entrance.

Entering, we found ourselves in another reality as soon as we crossed the threshold. Before us was a current of energy that flowed like the waters of a river; but it was not water. It was a river of diaphanous energy that shimmered and ran over a bed of round stones, forming whirlpools.

An old wooden boat waited for us against a rock. The Ageless Woman stepped inside, took the oars, and sat down. Smiling, she invited me to sit across from her. As I did so, she began to row through that electric flow.

"The waters of life," said the Agelesss Woman, "existed before the water of the Earth. They will take us far."

Her words intrigued me, but I said nothing, and she did not elaborate. The waters of life branched into narrower and narrower currents, the vegetation around us becoming thicker and more dense, until it became a tropical jungle. Animal

Remembrance

sounds emanated from all directions.

After a while, the Ageless Woman rowed us to a bank.

"We have arrived," she said, as we touched the bank's edge.

She stepped out of the boat and indicated that we would continue on foot. I was afraid, but followed her, carefully watching my steps. We kept close to the bank; the soil was slightly wet and soft, as if after a rainfall. We passed by lush green plants growing under the canopy of tall, broad trees. Vines snaked around them, covered in bright orange and yellow blossoms. I could hear the screeches of monkeys and the songs and calls of birds, the whirr of their wings.

A little farther, I saw plants and animals that I knew did not live in a tropical forest, trees that came from colder climates, a mink, and even a caribou. Slowly, the weather cooled. What I had taken for a jungle was far more complex than I had previously thought.

"In the waters of life, everything is possible," the Ageless Woman said, as if answering my thoughts.

"We are in the jungle of metamorphosis; the waters of life bathe and feed it. It is the Eden of love, a place with representatives from the whole story of life on Earth, and still more. We will spend some time and camp here," she said.

She pointed to an open area and handed me a blanket that I had not known she had brought. The sun was setting. It had been a long day, and I was feeling tired; I covered myself with the blanket and the vision ended.

Chapter Twelve
Liquid Love

When I next opened my eyes, the sun could barely pass through the copious vegetation around me. I looked for the Ageless Woman. She was a short distance away, observing the exuberant scenery around us.

"This Jungle was not always this large," she said as she sat down by my side, "nor did it always hold such a variety of plants and animals. Rather, it grew little-by-little as the different beings appeared on Earth. There was a time when only the first form of sentient life lived here."

The Ageless Woman then began to share a story. As she spoke, the images of what she explained appeared before me.

"At first, this new life was just a simple, ethereal, dynamic, electric light. It was imperceptible to the naked eye. Despite its simplicity, it was extremely powerful, because it was gifted with three attributes—a memory, an inner order, and a special capacity for growth.

"The memory was comprised of four remembrances: remembrance of its origins in the invisible universe; remembrance of its unity with all existence; remembrance of its function on the planet; and remembrance of its innate wisdom to perform that function. Its order was to live, to be. Its capacity was the potential to develop into infinite forms of life in the world.

"Slowly, a layer made of diverse earthly and cosmic substances began to surround, penetrate, and mold this light into a shape. As it grew more dense, it covered and obscured the original light, until that light was almost entirely obscured or unnoticeable in its material sheath. Nevertheless, the sheath remained capable of translucence, as if echoing its origins."

I understood that the new life was a cell that lived in the waters of the Earth.

"The arrival of this sentient being initiated a new beginning and changed the planet. In the beginning of the beginning, the divine source was all there was, and its love for itself was infinite and unconditional. This is why all creations are manifestations of its love.

"But when the first sentient being came into existence, it was so tiny, so very small, that its structure was incapable of manifesting the vastness of such love. It expressed as much as it could, but the rest of that infinite love remained latent inside it.

"Thus, the capacity to express love divided into two: the sentient being embodied and expressed love for itself; its surroundings—the waters of the Earth—manifested the unconditional, infinite love.

"One day, this tiny being feared that if it died, its form of life would disappear. It felt the need to beget offspring. Since it was alone, it offered its own life to create a new one, dividing itself, as the unity of the source had self-divided into the uncreated and the created.

"With this birth, and all the births that have followed it, the continuity of life was assured in the material universe, where everything was constant impermanence and transformation.

"The newborn was received, cared for, and transported by the water that acted as mother and father, providing it a home. At the same time, having had access to the innate wisdom of love from birth, this being was not dependent on any other for its own survival."

As the Ageless Woman spoke these words, I saw a twinkling light appear over me. The light descended and entered my head. I could sense movement—slow and watery. This sensation gradually became an ocean of crystalline water, covered by

Liquid Love

a golden substance, a mantle infused with the colors of the rainbow. Something told me that this substance was love, and the colors were the many forms it could manifest in the world.

The mantle of love split, forming two wings. One plunged into the water, which became saturated with love as the wing dissolved. The other transformed into a veil that expanded over the ground and up into the sky, like the rays of sunlight at dawn.

The edge of this veil dove into the waters made of love and curled slightly, creating what looked like a nest. That nest embraced and held the brilliant and translucent cell while the waters rocked and carried it from one place to another. The nest began to stretch, giving more room to the cell as it divided into countless tinier cells that soon rejoined each other.

Remembrance

Thus, a body began to take shape. Soon after, a thick, hard shell covered it. It looked similar to abalone. A current of water began to push the animal softly but firmly, again and again. The force of the current entered the body of the animal, which started to move on the ocean floor by itself, slowly.

An animal, like the one recently formed, approached it. Both of them emitted a substance into the water, and the two substances combined to create a new cell. The edge of the golden veil enveloped the new cell, and it began to change and transform 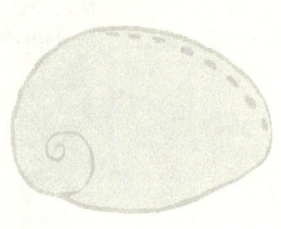 until it had a tail and fins. It was a fish that swam fast; its body was thin and long and illuminated with a dazzling reddish light.

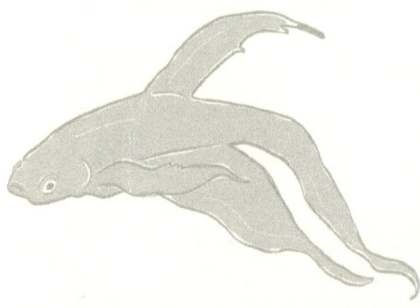 I had already noticed this light, but had not yet focused on it. However, it now had my attention, because I realized that this blood-red color was the wisdom of love activated, which allowed the creature to care for itself, from birth.

The water surrounded, held, and gave the being a home. Then the veil of love enveloped the fish, while its body transformed again. It grew legs, pulled its head out of the water, and with a leap reached the land!

I heard a potent repeating croak—a call for union.

This song attracted a mate.

Afterward, the mother frog laid a large number of small eggs against a rock and carefully covered them with a foamy substance from her own body, as if the water's love had begun to manifest through her.

Liquid Love

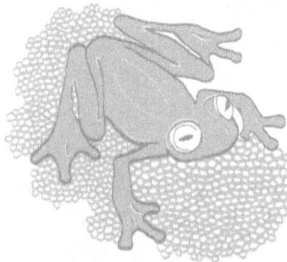

A moment later, the wing that had dissolved in the water became a huge wave that covered the land and shot through the air, so that everything was drenched and infused with love. The golden veil surrounded the mother frog, and her body acquired a thicker skin, similar to armor, and a new animal, a turtle, crawled away from the water.

The turtle made a hole in the ground and delicately laid larger and more solid eggs than the previous ones. Before leaving them, she covered them with sand. I saw in this hole a kind of womb; in that darkness, the necessary protection for life before coming out into the light.

The love of the vast waters of the Earth had become a liquid inside the egg that covered and nurtured the unborn baby. Soft rays of sunlight warmed the nest made of sand and matured the baby inside the egg. There was an intimate relationship between the sun and the Earth, and life in the world was a response to that union.

Then the veil of love surrounded one of these eggs, which gained hardness and resistance, and was now in a nest of leaves, twigs, and straw. It was protected by its mother's feathered body, which shone with not only a reddish light, but also a yellowish color, as if the warmth of the sun—the warmth love—had taken on her shape.

From the egg, a little chick was born; it was thin, bald, and unable to provide for itself, but with a loud voice, it called for food. Its father immediately flew over the nest, left, and a little later returned with food. The mother stayed with her chick,

Remembrance

placed food in its mouth, and covered it with her wings. Later, when the baby ventured out of the nest, she taught it how to fly.

In a way, the intelligence of the self-preservation of love, which had been innate in other species, was now dividing: it was, on the one hand, the pressing needs of the chick, and on the other, a caring and protective response in the parents. The more love the baby received, the more it learned to care for itself, and the stronger the yellow light of the sun shone in its chest.

I saw another hard-shelled egg. The golden veil that covered it expanded. The egg began to transform and travel from the outside into the interior of a mother covered by soft fur, which radiated with a red, yellow, and blue luminescence. The mother was a she-wolf that lived with her pack. At one point, she left the pack, entered a dark wooded area, and lay down behind a small pile of fallen branches and leaves. Her body tensed with spasms, and she gave birth to her pup.

I saw the she-wolf clean her pup with her tongue, shelter it with the warmth of her fur, and nurture it with her milk. With an attentive and selfless love, she taught her pup to survive. Together they returned to the pack. Under the vigilant eyes of

its mother, the curious pup explored its surroundings, imitating her. As it learned, a sky-blue light that circled its head glowed more and more brightly.

The veil stretched as the flow of love increased. The colors grew brighter and combined until becoming a brilliant white light, and a last image formed of a human being. This vision lasted only seconds, but before fading, it left a message in my heart—*Love is the universal nest; love is all that exists.*

Liquid Love

When I opened my eyes, it was still dark. I moved quietly, trying not to make a noise; but as I stood up, I saw that the Ageless Woman was awake, too, not far from our camp. I walked toward her and she looked at me with a smile. She pointed to the other side of the waters of life to some plum trees that had just bloomed. The vivid white-pink color of the buds contrasted with the dense foliage of the jungle.

"Life on Earth," she said, "is transformation, a continuous metamorphosis. These variations of the natural world are needed to free the wisdom of infinite love. Love travels through the physical universe. Freedom is gained through matter. The cycle of existence is an endless circular and spiral movement, where unity divides, multiplies, and returns to unity; but this new unity is different from the original. Each species can manifest a certain amount of love, but also, incorporates and expresses a certain amount of the essence of the forces of nature."

In this way, she made me realize that she was aware of my vision, even though I had said nothing about it.

Chapter Thirteen
Fear

One morning, the Ageless Woman picked up a brown pebble and threw it into the river of energy. While sinking, the stone made ripples that, little by little, revealed a marine tableau. The waters were calm. Fish of different sizes and colors came and went. In the shallow areas, there were sea anemones and starfish against the rocks; a turtle was swimming through seaweed. Following the rhythm of the current, some squid and seahorses passed by and, going in the opposite direction, an octopus disappeared into the deep.

Suddenly, the waters became agitated; animals began to chase and attack each other. The larger ones ate the smaller. But the weaker ones did not give up easily; they camouflaged themselves in the seabed, swam at great speeds, hid inside their shells, veiled behind colored inks that tinted the water. All the animals were in a state of alarm. I could smell their fear; it permeated the whole place.

"At the core of all earthly beings, there is a powerful call, a call to exist. In a universe of duality," the Ageless Woman explained, "this call is born with a twin—the fear of extinction.

"This fear increased the marine animals' attention and dedication to their own protection and survival, awakening their need to preserve themselves above everything else. Self-preservation is a fundamental expression of love for oneself, and it is essential for the continuity of life. But outside of the real needs expressed by this basic instinct, the desire to preserve oneself above everything else can become a distortion that harms others."

Remembrance

The Ageless Woman paused now and looked upward. As she did so, a flock of geese in a V-formation crossed the sky.

"The journey of love through matter," she continued, "is a journey toward the infinite. It does not end with the love of oneself; but rather, continues toward universal and unconditional love. Through the different expressions of life on Earth, an ever vaster and more embracing love has been embodied until, reaching the human being, it finds the capacity of loving infinitely, and of *knowing* that it loves infinitely."

The biblical phrase, "Love your neighbor as yourself," sounded in my mind.

"Universal love is a love that does not see anything as 'other'; it is a love that is beyond the duality of oneself and one's neighbor, beyond fear," the Ageless Woman said, responding to my thoughts once again. "This love is a gift from the most elevated heights of the soul—the angelical consciousness.

"When one feels universal love, the protection of oneself becomes the protection of the One, of all Life; and the love for oneself becomes love for the One, for everyone and everything, because this love knows that we are actually One."

We continued walking along the banks of the waters of life. After sunset, we slowly ascended a knoll. When we arrived at the top, the stars glimmered like diamonds against dark velvet. The crisp, clean air gave the vaulted skies a remarkable depth. I felt that I was inside the sky and part of its vastness. Little by little, the moon rose and shone over us; it was incredibly beautiful. Its greyish spots made it look like a serene and illuminated face. We sat on a tree trunk to wait for the dawn.

Chapter Fourteen
Queen of the Sky

"People used to call the moon the queen of the sky and mother of the Earth," the Ageless Woman said as the full moon was washed away by the rays of the rising sun.

Never before had I heard the moon described this way; but I thought it made sense.

"In those days," she continued, "her power was understood. She influenced everything—the rhythms of the waters of the planet, certain cycles in human life, the flow of dreams, and some of the patterns in them. The moon's presence is fundamental for the life of the world and its people; although not many know it because her power affects them without their noticing it.

"The queen of the sky was the first cosmic teacher. Her phases taught human beings the secret of transformation and the cyclical pattern of life. Her phases showed them the nature of time and a way to measure it.

"The night revealed the mystery of the beginning of life in darkness—the seed underground, the baby in the womb, the offspring in the egg. The stars displayed the great map of the universe and a way to orient oneself in the world; and dreams, the messengers of the night, unveiled their wisdom and guided people on their journeys."

I responded, "I recall reading once that in dreams the moon was interpreted as a symbol of the feminine."

"In the distant corners of memory," the Ageless Woman said, "the moon continues to be the queen of the sky. She symbolizes humanity's original wisdom—that natural, internal, feminine way of knowing the cadence and cycles of nature and life, a wisdom that arrives as a sensation, as a 'gut feeling,' without thinking.

"Because the moon lives together with the stars and other celestial bodies in the night sky, she also represents the inherent understanding of the interrelation and unity of all life. In this union, there is no 'you' or 'I,' but only 'we,' where nothing is separated from the whole.

"With time, however, the brilliance of the sun overshadowed the moon. She lost her sovereignty; and the sun who used to be her husband, and the Earth's father, became the king supreme.

"There were reasons for this. The sun reigned supreme during the day and people saw it as the the source of life. They began to associate it with being awake, and the moon with being asleep. The moon's light was cold, and the sun's light warm; thus fire was seen as a gift from the sun-king, which gave people the warmth the night lacked.

"Little by little, this symbol of the masculine, was associated with consciousness—the sense of an individual self, human discernment, and the worlds of light and things positive—while the lunar symbol of the feminine began to be associated with the unconscious, the undifferentiated, the unknown, the occult, and the negative."

When she had finished speaking, we returned to the camp. The sun was sinking below the treetops. It got colder and we made a fire to keep warm. The croaking of frogs became louder, and as I listened to them, I felt a deep and inexplicable sadness, a sharp pain in my chest.

The Ageless Woman noticed how I was feeling and said: "Love is the greatest force of cohesion that exists. Love is continuously trying to reunite that which was separated, and uses every possible means of attraction to accomplish that reunion—from the human longing to merge with the infinite, to the call of union in these animals. The created seeks to unite with the uncreated to feel whole again."

The Ageless Woman looked beautiful, illuminated by the moonlight from above, and by the fire near us. Her eyes were like pools without end. Observing her, I remained thoughtful. I did not yet know the name of this woman who read my thoughts, created images out of nowhere, and who took me to other worlds.

"I cannot reveal my name," she said. "Throughout time, I have been called by many names, though few have actually ever wanted to know my name."

Chapter Fifteen
Bliss

A few days later, I accompanied the Ageless Woman to collect berries from some nearby bushes. We returned to camp loaded with fruit. I grabbed some and lay down under the sun while eating one after another. The heat of the sun and my full stomach relaxed my body. I closed my eyes, ready to meditate, when I felt a warmth in my heart. It was not the warmth of the sun on my chest. It was like a caress or a very delicate tickling. Then, a deep bliss flooded my whole body.

I knew this feeling. It was the happiness of Earth. I had felt it before; but this time, it was much more intoxicating. I opened my eyes and looked around. The same joy permeated the air and everything around me. It was in the vivid color of the ivy, in the energy of the waters of life, in the song of the birds, and the smell of the berries. It was the bliss of existence, and it saturated everything.

The Earth was completely alive. She was intelligent. I could feel how she experienced her life through her body. Each being gave her a particular experience, a new sensation, a distinct emotion. My feelings were her feelings, my thoughts her thoughts. The ecstasy made me want to jump and laugh and run.

I looked at the Ageless Woman, who now looked very old, and she said to me: "This bliss you are radiating is the light of the soul shining through you."

I could only smile. I could not speak. I went up to her and lay my head on her lap. The Ageless Woman caressed my hair sweetly, and then explained: "When one connects with the

Remembrance

happiness of life, one connects with one's own soul, and with the soul of the world. Joy is the fiber of all, the music of the universe, the current in the air one breathes, and the essential quality of life.

THE THIRD PASSAGE:
Interconnection

"The interconnection of all life is very real; and yet, frequently it is not perceived by the naked eye."
  — The Ageless Woman

Chapter Sixteen
A Secret Garden

A few days later, we took the same path that led to the berry bushes; but halfway there, the Ageless Woman took a footpath flanked by thick foliage. Soon the leafy canopies of the trees hid the light of the sun and we were surrounded by the deafening buzz of insects. The heat coated my forehead with sweat, and my body felt sticky from the viscous humidity. This part of the jungle was a real tropical forest. Gradually, the path began to be covered by plants until it completely disappeared. My senses sharpened, became alert, and my breathing accelerated.

"There is always a way," the Ageless Woman said serenely, "One only needs to pay attention, listen to the sounds, observe the trees and other plants; nature will indicate where to go."

We continued heading inland until we reached a narrow stream and then followed the stream-bed. The soothing running and dripping of water amongst stones and roots drowned-out much of the jungle's other 'voices' and started to calm my fear. Unexpectedly, a clearing formed and everything became utterly silent. It was as if we had entered a large bubble of silence, a clear area by a small lake open to the sky. With a gesture, the Ageless Woman indicated to me to sit.

The waters of the lake were perfectly still. They reflected the clouds with precision. A leaf fell, and I could hear the soft swish of it in the air. A bird took flight and the sound of its wings flapping reverberated in my ears. The ground became gradually more and more transparent, until I found myself sitting on a translucent glass that revealed everything below us: countless minuscule stones and clumps of soil, a multitude of narrow subterranean tunnels made by small animals and

Remembrance

insects, numberless roots that meshed with each other forming a web. An inner universe, deep and secret, was suddenly unveiled before me.

Above ground, the contours of plants began to blur, and a luminous energy emanated from each one of them until it joined them all together, like a great living web. The clearing glowed and became completely united by roots below and light above, creating one single organism made of matter and energy. An even deeper silence flooded everything. I felt infinitely small, and I saw nature as a goddess—magnificent, awe-inspiring, and perfect.

I realized that since the beginning of my journey, the Earth had been uncovering more and more of her essence, as if she were undressing and showing me aspects of herself that were unknown to me. Slowly, the ground regained its opacity, and the bodies of plants had their own shape again. These successive transformations enthralled me.

Something moved among the tall grasses, the water swirled in the middle of the lake, and a strange soft breeze blew. I noticed that the breeze was becoming visible and made of tiny moving points which turned into little lights.

Suddenly, as if someone had pulled back a curtain, I saw small beings of different sizes and appearances that were causing the movement in this environment. Concentrating on their tasks, they did not notice us. Some took care of the water, cleaning it, others distributed seeds and placed little pebbles in particular spots on the ground. Two of them climbed a tree and were fixing bird nests. Most of them, however, nursed the plants: they tended the herbs, the wildflowers, and the trees around us. Their movements were precise and loving, and had a certain rhythm. They not only worked for nature, they communicated with it.

At one point, what seemed like a very large piece of transparent muslin descended and laid over them all. The little beings put their duties aside. It was as if that muslin was caressing them. It stayed in place for a moment and ascended again. As soon as it was gone, everyone returned to work. A little later, the breeze of tiny lights returned, closed the curtain to that world, and disappeared. "The little lights were fairies," said the Ageless Woman as we left the clearing. "Both the fairies and the beings that cared for the environment belong to a family that your world calls 'elementals.' They live in an ethereal planetary dimension.

"The elemental plane comprises a large number of workers and servants of the planet. Most of these operate in teams. Whether one sees them functioning together (like the fairies) or on their own (like those taking care of the different plants or attending to the earth), each of them is part of a larger working-group that cares for and is in charge of tending to a particular kind of animal, plant, or mineral.

"The job of 'devas' "—by which the Ageless Woman seemed to mean 'guardian' or 'protector,' the soul of a species or a forest—"is more solitary. Some of them, like the one that descended over the group, act as guides. The most powerful ones can be in charge of a whole forest. There was a time, forgotten by the people of your time, when the elementals worked with humanity. But the relationship became muddied when humans abused their connection with this realm. Only a cycle later, humanity began to connect positively with the elemental universe again. This time, the humans did not attempt to have the elementals at their service, but wanted to collaborate to protect life on Earth."

Having access to this reality changed something in me, and I began to experience the flora of the jungle in a new way. I became attuned to the acute sensitivity of plants, that intelligence which let them sense each other, perceive the closeness of an animal, or us, as well as let them know where to find what they needed to live.

We went back by a different path and passed a huge old tree. Its trunk towered so high it seemed to touch the sky. Its mighty size emanated a tremendous power. Some of its thick lateral roots protruded from the ground forming natural seats. I felt invited to lie down and rest on one of them. The tree's

Remembrance

bark was thick and hard, but it was speckled with ferns and mosses, which made it softer. The branches were home to many animals, and the rays of the sun gave the dark green of the leaves a metallic sheen. Lying on this protruding root, I breathed in deeply, filling my lungs with the moist clean air of the place.

Little by little, I became aware of how my breathing connected me with the breath of the tree and the rest of the forest, how the coming and going of our inhalations and exhalations were a dance that wove a web of breath. I united with the jungle, merged with it, and was led inward to a soundless, peaceful place, bathed by a warm and faint light. A force that I did not know took my whole being. I felt as if I were a plant.

The vitality that ran throughout my body was the Earth's energy, of the ground where I was rooted. I felt as if my feet were diving deep into that ground and absorbing nutrients. My arms seemed to spread out, searching for sunlight. Everything was silence and sensation. I experienced the joy of total surrender. The plant I had become felt the happiness of giving itself, and in doing so, of serving life.

Gradually, I returned to my own body and the jungle's reality, to its colors, shapes, and sounds. I got up and continued onward with the Ageless Woman.

The many experiences of that day left me in an introverted state. Traveling with the Ageless Woman meant accessing the extraordinary, and coming into contact with the miraculous dimension of the world in each moment.

"What I lived today," I said to the Ageless Woman, "gave me palpable proof of the interrelation and unity of all life."

"The interconnection of life is very real; and yet, like the underlying sibling-hood of plants, and the sense of unity and communion of the elementals with the natural world, it is frequently hidden from the naked eye," she responded.

Chapter Seventeen
Drops of the Great Soul

We passed by an area covered by aromatic shrubs that smelled strongly of mint.

"Due to their high sensitivity and subtlety," said the Ageless Woman, "plants fulfill a particular function for the Earth's life—they are the natural cleaners and healers of the planet. Plants are incredibly generous. Their bodies absorb the negativity in the world and purify it. They are shelter to many animals, give medicines, and give their lives to feed others. And when they fulfill their cycle of existence, they revitalize the body of the planet."

Her words made me aware that I had rarely considered how the soil under our feet is made of the bodies of plants, animals, and human beings.

"The soil is an outer planetary layer," she said, "a reservoir that collects beings' physical bodies when they transition. In it, the substances disintegrate and transform until they become an integral part of this layer. In addition, there are numerous ethereal layers surrounding the planet, such as the layers of sensation, and thoughts.

"Once a plant transitions, its body becomes part of the layer of soil, and the sensations it experienced during its life on Earth return to the reservoir of sensations. Likewise, when an animal transitions, its physical body merges into the layer of the Earth's outer layer, while its feelings return to the reservoir of feelings, and its mind to the reservoir of instinctual intelligence.

Remembrance

"The story of the world lies in these layers—the collective memory, the chronicles, the powers and weaknesses of the gods and goddesses of antiquity. Each layer has a specific planetary function and comprises a part of the memory of the world and a wisdom, a particular form of knowledge.

"These levels not only serve as reservoirs, but also function as 'dressing-rooms' for souls.

"When a soul is to inhabit the Earth, its naked body is dressed with the substances of the different planetary layers. These 'clothes' serve the soul for its purpose during its stay on the planet, and when it leaves, it gives them back.

"Occasionally, these garments can undergo changes due to the being's experiences and the realizations it has reached. So, in a way, the 'dressing-rooms' are continually changing and renovating.

"The greatest of all 'dressing rooms' is the great soul, the first layer of creation and infinite love, whose function is to clothe the spirit of life and give birth to all the other physical and ethereal layers that exist in the universe.

"The great soul is like an infinite ocean, in which, each being's soul, no matter how large or small, is a tiny drop. Since each drop of the great soul is made of love and wisdom, like the great soul, each layer of reality is, too. And since each being is made of a certain number of layers, love is the being itself.

"Once 'disrobed,' having returned all that it has learned, the drop dissolves and merges with the oceanic great soul, forgetting itself and falling asleep. Through the individual experience of each drop, and the knowledge it acquired about itself, the great soul knows itself ever more profoundly and evolves.

"The more conscious and awake the incarnated soul-drop becomes, the more individualized it is; a granule forms within that begins to gain a certain vivacity that inures to it. While the rest of the drop dissolves and merges in the immensity of the

Drops of the Great Soul

great soul, this granule does not forget itself fully, but remains awake in the immensity."

I asked the Ageless Woman if the living recollection of that awakened granule of soul related in some way to reincarnation.

She answered, "The soul and its different sheaths or layers reincarnate."

"Since all the drops of soul dissolve what they have learned in the great soul's infinite ocean and the different 'dressing-rooms,' each incarnating drop is new, in a certain way. Each soul-drop is a specific mix of a few experiences, characteristics, and learning of the great soul and the different layers. This is why those who access the memories of their soul usually contact the fragments of the memories of that layer.

"The awakened granules can bring memories of their own past, but the person who accesses them often forgets them as the personality gains strength.

"One of the functions of human incarnation is to improve the quality of the Earth's layers consciously. Human beings do this through the cultivation of good thoughts, pure feelings, and well-intentioned actions.

"The great soul is comprised of veils or sub-layers with different degrees of density. In the most ethereal and nearest veil to the uncreated spirit, everything dissolves. The few awakened granules inhabit the following veils.

"As the veils gain density, certain formations, clusters, or bunches, appear; and later, within the clusters, in even denser layers, are located groups, families, and sub-families of drops.

"The drops of a particular family, or drops who share a common destiny, are related. So it is possible that they are born close to each other, or that they belong in the same blood-family, or that life-circumstances bring them together.

"The journey of a soul-drop is a journey toward the nothingness of the uncreated. But many times, as it disincarnates, the drop cannot get there, and instead, remains within the clusters or families from where it departed.

Remembrance

"Thus, another kind of reincarnation occurs, one based on the common elements individual drops share, such as the need to learn something specific, or the need to repeat a particular experience in a new way, or even end something unfulfilled."

Chapter Eighteen
Magic Memory

One morning, referring to the enormous tree that we had seen shortly before, the Ageless Woman said, "Trees are silent witnesses of the events around them. They carry the memory of the history of the world and of humanity. This is their magical quality.

"Magic and its qualities come from the immaterial worlds and manifest themselves through dense matter. It was the magic of life that made something as memorious as trees to come into existence from the first sentient being. It was this same miraculous act that made that first being incarnate on Earth," she added.

Then, observing a rock covered with moss by the waters' banks, she continued, "The Earth wants to know her own totality. Responding to that need, sentient life has sought to propagate itself to cover her. Thus, slowly, it inhabited the waters, the grounds, and the planet's air through fins, legs, wings, and seeds."

As she finished saying these words, a vast green prairie appeared before us. A strong wind was blowing. Then it calmed down and a rain of seeds began to fall. Some descended, spinning quickly, while others swayed slowly, and some, as thin as needles, flew away, pushed by the breeze. Everywhere, there were flakes with small brown seeds floating down.

The prairie became multicolored—red, yellow, purple, white, pink, and orange flowers covered the ground and permeated the air with joy and the smell of spring.

Remembrance

The Ageless Woman began to walk, then turned toward me and made a sign for me to follow. In the middle of the prairie, I saw a tree, full of little white flowers with yellow centers, its branches laden with fruit, some ripe, and some still green. Bees and hummingbirds flew from flower to flower, absorbing their sweetness.

I was observing one of these flowers closely when it started to change, becoming a fruit connected to the tree by a short stem. Somehow, I was able to see the interior of the fruit; there, the seed was surrounded and protected by a soft substance. I saw the seed inside the fruit as if in a womb and linked to the rest of the mother plant's body by an umbilical stem; it revealed to me the close parallels between the evolution of the different realms of life.

A moment later, the tree emitted a strong fragrance, exquisite, that attracted more bees, and some large birds that began to eat the ripe fruits. I noticed a particular pleasure that the tree felt in feeding others and being served at the same time.

"Life is a vast web that unites all beings," said the Ageless Woman, "all creations, big and small, visible and invisible. Although there are many forms of connections, groups, and associations—some evolving, others regressing—the web of mutual help is fundamental for the development of the planet.

"Without it," she said as the prairie disappeared, "the Earth of the bearers of remembrance cannot be reached."

Part Four:
Awakening

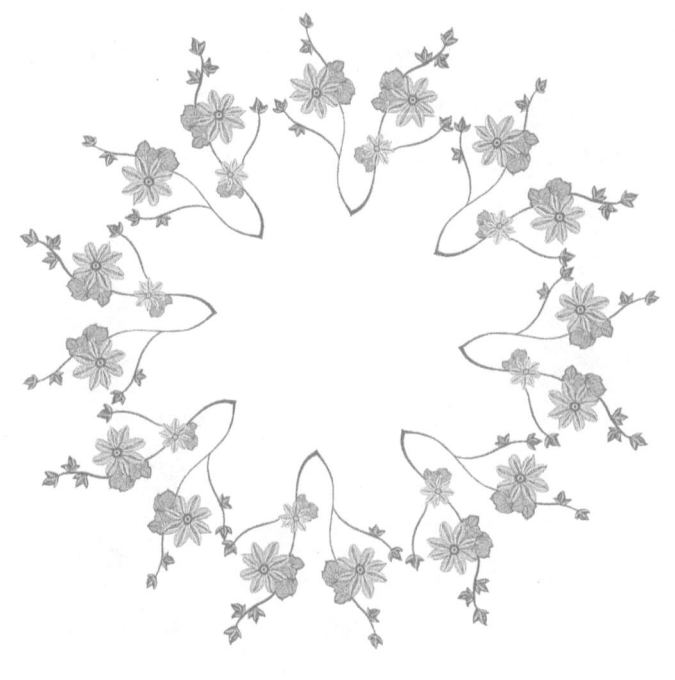

Chapter Nineteen
The Human Being

One afternoon, when I was resting by the waters of life, the Ageless Woman came up to where I was, sat by my side, opened her hand, and showed me a green marbled stone the size of a quail's egg. I knew she would throw it into the waters; she wanted to teach me something.

While sinking, the stone formed ripples of energy, which created the image of a large luminous sphere that levitated over the waters of life. The sphere was made of many layers, like an onion.

The Ageless Woman said, "There is another story of creation that affirms that the whole of existence is a great sphere. This great sphere became known as the 'mother cell,' the multi-dimensional cell of life. It is a single sphere, and each of its inner layers is a universe."

A rhythmical movement of contraction and expansion, similar to a heartbeat, started in the mother cell's central layer. The movement began to strengthen and expand, pushing the other layers outward and enlarging the sphere until, at some point, a new one arose from the middle of this central layer.

"It is the physical universe," the Ageless Woman said, pointing to it. The large sphere of the mother cell then began to turn, allowing me to see its interior. The layers looked like hollow weaves of wool, all of different thicknesses.

"Nothing can exist outside of the whole," she added.

The scene dissolved and, in its place, the image of a human being emerged. This human being slowly became an oblong cell made of many layers, similar to the mother cell's, but of smaller size and with three of the layers—the outer, the middle, and the central one—more visible than the others. The outer layer was made of a brilliant translucent light. The middle one had more consistency and was opaque and smaller than the layer of light. The layer at the core of the cell was a little hole and the smallest of all. All the layers seemed connected: they were inter-dependent.

"The outer layer," the Ageless Woman said, "is the layer of the soul. The second is the physical body, and the central layer is the void. The others are sub-layers—intuitions, thoughts, feelings, and vital energies, among others."

The three more visible layers began to intertwine and change sizes and positions in such a way that, at times, the layer of the physical body covered the layer of the soul, and at other times, the void became larger than the other two.

"Like the mother cell, each human being is a multi-dimensional cell made of various layers and sub-layers. Each layer corresponds to a dimension of existence or non-existence.

"The physical body is made from the particles of the material cosmos, and is home to the instinctual nature. The soul's layer belongs to the universe of celestial beings, and is home to unconditional, infinite love. The layer of emptiness comes from the universe of the uncreated and is home to nothingness.

"In the cell of the human being, the layers interweave because they interpenetrate each other."

The Ageless Woman made a sign with her pointing finger, and a swirl was formed in the river of energy that absorbed the image of the human cell.

As we walked and talked together in this way, days passed. My experience of life was changing. Nothing was like before.

The Human Being

I could see another face of things, one with deep meaning, where nothing was 'just because.' Everything had a purpose. I could feel nature talking to me, telling me her secrets. My heart was open. I was relaxed, content. Often, I felt as if I were a newborn or an infant. I experienced each thing as if it was new. Even if I could recall having seen or done something before, it was as if it were for the first time. I did not understand entirely how that happened, but it filled me with joy.

I could sense that the Ageless Woman had noticed this change in me and knew how I felt. Still, she said nothing about it until, one morning, after we had been walking in silence for several hours through a forest of deciduous trees, far from the waters of life, she slowed her pace and said—"When one lives in the present moment, it is always new. The present moment is outside of time, where there is neither past nor future."

After she said this, we walked on in silence among the trees and the many ferns growing under their shade. The silence gave me space to ponder the words I had just heard.

The Ageless Woman paused then and directed my attention to a red squirrel with a white belly and a long bushy tail that was carefully building her nest on the branch of a tree. As soon as the squirrel saw us, she stopped to observe us for a brief moment, and then climbed to a higher and thinner branch. Glancing sideways and moving her ears towards each new sound and to our movements, the squirrel selected a few stems with fresh leaves, broke them off, and placed them against the nest's walls.

"Almost all life on Earth exists without consciousness of time," said the Ageless Woman. "Among humans, it is only as they grow that they develop a conscious awareness of linear time, of past and future. When they are very young, humans live out of time, like this beautiful squirrel," explained the Ageless Woman as we sat at a distance not to disturb her. Then she added, "There is a difference between living in the present moment consciously and unconsciously. Living it consciously is a particular state of being, an aspect of soul-consciousness.

Remembrance

The more the temporal reality prevails, the more the present moment gets lost."

We watched how the squirrel worked, coming and going, reinforcing the nest's walls for a long while. The sun was going down when we bid her goodbye. We left talking about her dedication to making the nest, and her love toward her future brood.

"Mother Earth continues creating beings that are ever more capable of living a vaster and greater unconditional love; the arrival of human beings on Earth brought the possibility that this could be experienced consciously."

I commented, "I cannot avoid feeling sad when I think that, before the appearance of humanity, so much time passed by when the beauty of the Earth was not perceived, when the existence of the world was unknown, and so much life came and went without anyone knowing it."

"It was and was not so," she responded. "A certain incorporeal prototype of the human being already existed. It existed as an idea, as a possibility, and as a goal in the subtle worlds.

"But that intangible presence was not enough to fulfill the function of humanity. A human being with a physical body was needed, because the importance of their creation relates to the rest of the natural world and the universe. Each forward step humanity takes offers a new possibility for the rest of the natural world to take a step forward as well. When the human being looks at the universe, the universe sees itself through their eyes.

"To build a suitable physical vehicle, capable of embodying a soul of the caliber of a human soul, would take a long time. The human being is not the only adequate vehicle for this soul, but is the best at this time on the planet.

"Human beings have qualities of the angelic and uncreated universes, but also gather aspects of the other beings of the Earth. They have body, sensations, feelings, emotions,

The Human Being

cognition—but they can also observe themselves and know they are doing this.

"This gives them the capacity to recognize the qualities that they share with the rest of the natural world, and to live them consciously in the name of all the other forms of life, which do not have this possibility. Their quality of consciousness is their gift to the planet, and what provides them with great creativity.

"When the time came for the arrival of human beings, when a vehicle was finally created that could contain this level of consciousness, there was a great celebration in the angelic world. Many angels offered to participate in the care and guidance of human beings, because human souls comprised a distinct, unique, and precious spark that would allow them to fulfill their mission in the universe. Humanity brought a new vibration of existence to the world, a new octave in the musical scale of life. That is why, since their arrival, they are cared for by protector angels."

Chapter Twenty
The Fabric of Love

A few nights later, another brilliant light appeared above my head, entered through my crown, and brought me a new vision.

There were people from all over the world and from different periods. Holding hands, they formed a belt around the planet. The golden veil of love emerged again and began to envelop each person. At the same time, an enormous human being called *"Humanity"* began to take shape, and each person in the 'belt' transformed into a cell of this being. One after the other, the veil wove all these cells together, until Humanity became a great golden fabric with a rainbow hue that radiated love on Earth.

A moment later, the cells began to unite, shaping the organs of the body of Humanity. In the heart of this colossal being, there was a particular light. I went toward it. When I was just a short distance from it, I saw two people embracing each other. The love that united them turned the golden veil that surrounded them pink.

Close-up, the light that had attracted me looked like a kind of cloud that glowed over the couple. An electric ray of light went through the couple's embrace, reached the woman's womb, and made visible its interior. There was a tiny cell—brilliant and transparent—held by the golden-rainbow veil of love and enlivened by the electric light.

Observing this cell, I was suddenly overcome with emotion. I realized that I was in the presence of a tremendous miracle of existence. Before me, veiled under the appearance of something seemingly small and insignificant, was an incarnated sliver of the divine. I saw that this little sliver carried the memory of the story of life and its relationship with the visible, the invisible, and the non-existent worlds. In it were the possibilities of human development, the characteristics of the new person, the history of its family and its ancestors.

Then the veil of love extended and covered the cell as it began to divide internally, over and over. It increased in size and nested firmly in the womb. The veil expanded again, and this new life began to turn and turn; each turn was a transformation of its body as it grew. At first, it looked like a fish, then a tadpole, and continued changing until, little by little, it acquired a human form.

Meanwhile, the cloud of shimmering light above the couple grew in intensity until it shone like a sun, exuding a palpable love. It was a holy light vibrating rhythmically in and out of the infant. The light was larger than its body. Each time the cloud entered the baby, she became radiant; and each time the cloud left the body, it remained united and connected to her through a single shining thread. This holy light was distinct from the electric energy that permeated and enlivened the baby from the beginning. It was also different from the light of other organisms I had seen. It was the light of the human soul.

It was as if the two worlds marked the infant: as her body grew and transformed, an imprint remained, a remembrance of its belonging to the Earth, an experience of the life of those beings that had opened the path to her existence. The light of her soul, and the electric energy of life that inhabited her body, were a stamp of its belonging to the invisible world.

I felt two presences entering the vision then. They were angelic beings. One of them lovingly and carefully embraced the infant. The other caressed the soul that inundated the little body and seemed to observe how it grew. The cord that united the infant with her mother was floating and looked very strong, a tube of connection and communication almost unbreakable.

The veil of love expanded again as the infant's body shifted and her head settled into the birth canal. The mother's womb

The Fabric of Love

began to contract, and the infant began its journey to birth.

I then saw the mother's naked body. As she pushed, her large round belly swelled and became an Earth, the Great Mother. She, too, was giving birth, bringing life, and her push was tireless, unstoppable.

The moon and the sky with its stars surrounded the mother Earth, and their presence carried a message of unity: the baby had been living in the waters of her mother, like the fish in the waters of the mother Earth, and there, the sky had too. That watery womb, where the light was dim and diffuse, was the night's domain, the queen-realm of the moon.

The sun illuminated the firmament, and I heard the baby's cry, an exclamation of joy. The cosmos was present, receiving her together with the angels emitting rays of love.

Slowly, the moon began to fade, the stars disappeared with the arrival of the day, and the sun shone radiantly in a light-blue sky. Being born was a first step toward the light of the sun.

A golden veil surrounded the mother, and she enveloped her newborn within her arms in a soft embrace. She brought her baby to her breast and began to feed her tenderly, and I saw in the milk the presence of the sky again, of the moon, a liquid created in the maternal breast's dark depths, and of the sun, for its warmth and the sweetness of its taste.

During breastfeeding, the hearts of the mother and the newborn began to beat as one, beaming pink rays of love that illumined them. The milk that flowed from her breast, home of the heart, also acquired a pink color. The baby drank from the breast, as if it were a shore of the waters wherein she had lived. At the same time, it offered the baby a place to rest her body, to root herself, and to be nurtured by this world. I saw that even while the cosmos and the invisible world completely loved the baby, it was physical contact, soft and caring, that gave her the experience of human love.

Remembrance

The Alchemy of Love

    A moment later, an edge of the veil of love expanded one more time. It glided along the infant's little arm as she placed it on her mother's chest, drawing my attention to a gold bracelet made of circular links on the infant's wrist. My vision focused on the bracelet and its links became larger and larger before my eyes; it became clear that they were not just hollow rings. The first link was a circle of a thin golden thread with a center of complete emptiness from whence emanated a tremendous power. This 'emptiness' began to pour part of itself into the next link, and there, the emptiness became a waterfall of infinite love, pure and transparent. This second link now contained this love. Then the love poured into a third link of the chain, and gave birth to another type of emptiness, the emptiness of outer space.

    Outer space was without end, even inside that little ring, and had an electric nature. Its vastness was overwhelming. Several galaxies floated in this space, among them the Milky Way. I felt pulled toward a tiny point of this galaxy located at the border of the link, at the intersection with the fourth one. As I moved closer, I realized that the little point was the Earth lit by the sun. Right beside her, the potent energy of outer space poured into the next link, where it became the vast waters of our planet.

    The fourth link also looked immensely vast. It held an ocean of clear waters that was home to many forms of life. I could feel how this ocean carried in its liquid the dynamic power of emptiness, the infinite quality of love, and the electric energy of outer space. And while it cascaded into the next link, a maternal womb, it transformed into the amniotic fluid surrounding an infant.

    This maternal amniotic fluid turned into a torrent, which, as it streamed into the sixth link, became the mother's milk. The nurturing substance, held in the last link of the infant's bracelet, carried within its sweet warmth a whole story of the alchemy

The Fabric of Love

of love. Where the milk slowly seeped into the emptiness of the first link, it formed a bridge between the finite and infinite, the created and the uncreated.

Chapter Twenty-One
The Path To Freedom

One day, the Ageless Woman asked me, "Do you remember the legend the Shepherdess told us about her people at the place of remembrance?"

"Yes," I said, "that beautiful story often comes to my mind."

"Let us continue that story," she said. "The bearers of remembrance discovered that all things were related, like links in a golden chain, that they too were a link, and this chain formed an infinite web that came from a single source.

"They further discovered that the source was pure emptiness enveloped by a layer of love, and that love is the soul and body of all things; that all creations, from the largest to the smallest link, carry within them the remembrance of their deep relationship with the other links, and with the source; and that they also tell the story of a journey, the journey of love through matter.

"They called this journey, 'the path toward freedom,' and understood that, since everything is made of love, the whole of life on Earth feels the need to move toward freedom. Realizing that they are made of infinite love, and reaching the freedom that this love brings, is part of human destiny.

"The birth of a baby in the world is a first step toward freedom. A newborn's arrival is a physical experience of absolute dependency. This dependency strengthens their call toward freedom and drives them to want to take control of their body and to provide for their own needs. Thus, in a relatively short period of time, a child acquires capacities and abilities which took the natural world and humanity eons to develop.

Remembrance

"By the time a baby is born, they have gone through several transformations in the aquatic home of their mother's womb. Then the day comes when they reach the coasts of the earthly world, and in a way, re-enact the moment long ago when the first animals and plants left the oceans and ventured on the surface.

"Just like those first animals and plants that had to live close to the waters, a newborn must initially remain close to the milk that nourishes them. Since newborns cannot transport themselves on their own, there is a continuous period of adaptation and rooting. Later, they stretch, gives themselves a push, start crawling and getting to know their home, as those first land animals and plants explored areas ever farther away from the large bodies of water of the Earth.

"Little by little, the baby becomes more and more independent. They begin to feed themselves, communicate with words, stand up and walk, then run and pass through and incorporate the stages of movement and communication of those that came before them."

Chapter Twenty-Two
The Source

Some days later, the Ageless Woman invited me to go for a walk. We crossed a bridge and heard a sound that became louder and louder while we moved forward. As we turned a corner, we saw a sparkling cascade of energy coming down from a rocky knoll and crashing forcefully into the riverbed below. We climbed a trail bordering the fall until we reached the top, where the current of energy was shallow. We followed this flow as it became narrower and narrower, until only a thread of it was left springing up between a small pile of rocks and a clump of short grasses. That was the origin of the waters of life.

"Everything has a source, and the source of the human being is their soul," said the Ageless Woman. "In a human being, the original quest for liberation is internal, and is born in their soul. When it frees itself, the soul becomes a spring of life, love, and wisdom, flowing through the physical body, just as this thread of energy bubbles up through this pile of stones.

"The human soul contains a spark of the divine spirit that arrives directly from the uncreated universe, and miraculously, unites with the soul that is common to all forms of life on Earth, embellishing it with this exceptional quality that makes it human.

"The soul remembers where it comes from, what it came to do, what it has to learn, and its essential qualities. It lives outside time, and knows its past and, to a certain degree, its future.

Remembrance

That is why the soul prepares itself with the dedication to come into the world and looks for a living circumstance that offers it the experience it needs to live. But it feels uncomfortable being limited by a physical body and not being understood. Despite this, it gives itself to live this experience in the world and surrounds and goes in and out of the body.

"The realm of the soul is an ethereal, pure, reality of unity and love. Reflecting this subtle nature, during gestation, the body of the baby is almost transparent; once born, their skin is thin, delicate, and perfumed, and their eyes have a watery and translucent shine.

"The unitive nature of the soul also manifests in various ways. Physically, this unity is seen when the baby is in the mother's womb, and when mother and child reunite through the mother's milk after birth. Energetically, the soul reveals itself through the creation of a strong ethereal egg that envelops mother and child and keeps them together.

"Before the layers of the personality are created, the soul can live its knowing of unity and vision of reality without much interference affecting the experience of life of the baby. The baby arrives in the world with an intrinsic and innate sense of unity that does not differentiate one thing from another. Thus, they experience their mother and the world as part of themselves, or as themselves.

"This state of union impacts the baby's destiny so much that, when they are cared for, they feel as though they are caring for themselves, and if they are hurt, they feel as if they are hurting themselves. They absorb everything around them as if it were food, even incorporating the thoughts and feelings of those who look after them as if they were their own.

"When a young child looks at the world through the eyes of the soul, everything is new, mysterious, and alive—a paradise full of miracles and a marvel. They are all of this and everything. But as they grow and begin to know the world around them better, the child's perception of being everything begins to fall

The Source

away. They realize that they are just one among many and see themselves as separate and different from others.

"At this time, they can still access the memories of their soul, and often dream and speak about them. Gradually, however, a little bit of their soul, the source of their unitive experience of life, begins to separate itself and becomes the child's personal identity. At the same time, the ethereal egg that had united them to their mother slowly begins to thin, giving the child a new sense of independence. "This change of perception awakens in a child the need to discover where *they* end, to understand what pertains to *them* and what does not, to know who *they* are. Thus, *their* notion of *self* emerges.

"As a child continues to grow, the child wants to know what life is all about, what things are made of, and how things really work. Their mind expands in many directions and acquires skills and knowledge, and the magical view of life weakens.

"The more they grow, the more their interests expand. They come in contact with new groups and incorporate their ways, ideals, beliefs, and knowledge. Thus, one after the other, they access different kinds of ethereal eggs, those of the circles to which they belong, and the ideas with which they associate.

"This results in greater personal development; but it also means that, little by little, their direct connection with an essential aspect of their nature diminishes. This awakens a longing in their soul to rebuild the strong bridge that once was."

Part Five:
Cycles

Chapter Twenty-Three
The Story of the World

Early the next day, the Ageless Woman began to cover the burned wood that remained from the fire with stones and wet earth. While helping her, I caught sight of the boat. I had not seen it in a while; it was floating by the bank not far from us.

"We are leaving," she said simply, noticing my glance.

It was painful to hear those words. They sounded hard, almost cold. I said nothing, but was choked with sadness. I folded my blanket and gave it to her. She placed it in the boat behind her seat, sat down, and signaled for me to get in and sit in front of her. I offered to help her row, but she said there was no need.

I knew I would not return to the jungle of metamorphosis. Internally, I said goodbye to the birds, the trees, the fire that had illuminated and warmed us, the elementals, the vibration of the waters of life.

The way back seemed too short. Soon we got out of the boat, took a few steps, and found ourselves back in the New Earth.

We took a trail we had taken before and passed by the sown fields while crossing the valley. The Ageless Woman's pace was slow and relaxed, and, as I walked behind her, the natural beauty of the area gradually diminished the sadness I was feeling.

We were getting close to town when we saw the Shepherdess leading her flock toward the mountains. The Ageless Woman said that we would meet her later at the place of remembrance.

Remembrance

When we arrived at the place of remembrance, the Shepherdess was sitting on the platform of the amphitheater, sharing a story with a few children gathered around her. After she finished her story and the children departed, we descended the steps and greeted her.

"I have been waiting for you," the Shepherdess said to us. She stood up and led us to another access to the amphitheater through a curved path that descended up to the mouth of a cave. She lit a torch that was close to the entrance and we passed slowly through the recesses of the grotto up to a flat space with seats carved into the rock and several baskets with dry fruits and large pitchers of water resting on the ground.

"We are underneath the plaque that marks the place of remembrance. Before building the amphitheater, our ancestors met here. The passing of time turned it into a sacred place of retreat and introspection. Here we come to reflect on the events that have marked our history."

"I will leave you now," said the Ageless Woman, and she took a few steps away from us, becoming gradually transparent. "I will return in a few days," she added while disappearing.

"During this time together, I will share with you the events that originated and brought an end to the period of the descent and how the world you see around you came to be," explained the Shepherdess, inviting me to sit next to her.

As I listened to her, I was flooded with images I had seen at the beginning of my journey: the time of the descent—rotting corpses, piles upon piles of trash, denuded forests, violent killings. My stomach tightened, and my heart sank. Noticing my discomfort, the Shepherdess paused for a moment before continuing.

"Our story unfolded in cycles," she said a bit later. "Each cycle brings a particular gift for the world, the development of life, and the evolution of human consciousness. There are greater and lesser cycles. The greater cycles last a long time, and their gifts reach the whole world. The lesser ones take place at specific times and places and serve as sparks for a greater change.

The Story of the World

"Aside from bringing along their innate characteristics and abilities, as human beings grow, they recreate and incorporate the advancements reached in the world during the greater and lesser cycles, until the moment and place of their birth and the time in which they live. Sometimes, though it is rare, not all of these advances are incorporated, or the advances of the future cycles are attained.

"The era of the *Descent* was not always called this," the Shepherdess continued. "Originally, it was known as the *Great Cycle of Differentiation,* a period that gifted the world with a powerful energy of change. Its arrival helped human beings to develop a notion of personal identity, individuality, and a capacity to choose freely. This transformed their vision of life.

"Previously, the human being, nature, and the divine, the visible and the invisible, the body and soul of all things, were intertwined and connected in an almost indistinguishable way. It was a world of instinctual, sensorial, and intuitive knowing that prioritized the collective and the sense of we.

"The great cycle of differentiation created a world of rational and deductive knowledge, where individual awareness, the unique, the distinct, and the sense of *I* and *you* prevailed.

"Some great cycles affect the world quickly. Others, like the cycle of differentiation, influenced the planet progressively. During this period, the perception of differences led to the observation of the finest distinctions among things, which resulted in incredible discoveries, inventions, and advancements in knowledge. The sense of a distinctive and separate identity also allowed an individual to develop their innate qualities and to live out the destiny of their essential nature—the destiny of their soul—consciously. This prepared the world for the next great cycle.

"But the natural course was altered; the cycle of differentiation became toxic. This toxicity lasted for thousands of years. It took over most of the planet, causing an imperceptible disruption in human understanding that disturbed and slowed the rooting of the next great cycle. This disruption made the sense of

Remembrance

differentiation a means of discrimination, and discrimination made people feel insecure about their own value.

"Increasingly, the cycle of differentiation turned into an era of confusion, uncertainty, and fear. This awakened such a need for personal security, value, and power, that it became difficult not to succumb to the desire to feel better and more powerful than others.

"This desire for power produced many forms of slavery. It was discovered that briefly satisfying a person's sense of security, value, and power, created a fear of losing it in them; through a constant evocation of that fear, a person's free will could be controlled. This knowledge spread rapidly over the world. All manner of attractions were produced, offering to eradicate these fears. This made many, without their noticing it, dependent on more and more of what was sold to them—people, activities, objects, concepts, substances, ideals.

"During that period, certain beliefs became rooted, which molded reality. It was a time when people bought more and more, believing that possessing material goods would make them happier and more powerful. To get the things they desired, many people labored to exhaustion each day; but did not always make enough to acquire all the things they desired. Sometimes what they earned was insufficient for even their basic needs. So, many people suffered hunger and misery. Deceit, theft, fraud, and other crimes became an everyday occurrence.

"People also believed in the power of weapons. More weapons meant more strength and security. There were cities with large armies that reigned over vast areas with the capacity to destroy all. There were thousands of years of revolts and revolutions, political, economic, and religious wars. Some people with power, influence, and persuasion, promoted these wars to sell weapons to all sides of these conflicts.

"With the idea of getting more and better for less, people exploited everything the Earth had to offer and discarded everything they did not use. Slowly, mountains and lands were

The Story of the World

destroyed, woods and jungles clear cut, air and water poisoned. The planet, in her way, complained and reacted, but her call fell on deaf ears. The Earth became an object to be bought and sold, used and discarded.

"Life became mechanized, personal contact and interaction disconnected. Anger and irritation escalated, and communication was increasingly expressed through insults, blows, and weapons. Prejudice and intolerance became the norm.

"This reality anguished, saddened, and sickened many. It led some to ignore what was happening, not to wanting to know what was going on. It led others to isolate themselves, alone or within groups. Still others spent as much time as possible distracting themselves, embracing forgetfulness. Gradually, the music of the Earth, the song life, stopped being heard."

As I listened to the Shepherdess, more images of the descent returned, the many events I saw, heard, and lived. I could not avoid crying again, but this time there was a difference. Previously, I had felt only pain, desperation, and frustration. Now, through the Shepherdess' words, I could see a deeper cause for our situation and began to understand what was taking place in my world.

The Shepherdess hugged me, and I gradually stopped crying. Her embrace made me feel understood.

Chapter Twenty-Four
Hope

The Shepherdess resumed her story the following day.

"To become aware is the first step toward change. Becoming conscious of something is an awakening. This awakening transforms our previous understanding and gives new meaning to our lives. It was the awareness of one person, then another, then another, and another, that eventually allowed the world to leave the period of the descent.

"Even as the situation became less and less tolerable, and more and more people believed that the reality of the descent was the only possible reality, losing any hope of a different life, there were still some who longed to be free, who wished to think on their own, who wanted to know who they were, where they came from, and where they were going. The answers they received from the descent did not satisfy them, so they sought to return to the source, to their true origin. To a large degree, this Earth owes its existence to their exploration."

After this, she fell silent.

Sometime later, I felt the need to be alone and told the Shepherdess that I would go for a walk. When I left the cave, the sun was near the horizon; its rays at the end of the day tinted the sky in red and orange. I felt like praying. Sitting on a rock, I closed my eyes and prayed for the Earth, for her people, for all her beings. I prayed for my family, and that my life, somehow, could make a difference.

Absorbed in prayer, I saw myself under a soft rain of golden sparks. The sparks came down from the sky like prisms, reflecting the sun's light, creating thousands of mirrors that inundated my heart with peace. I then heard a soft voice that

Remembrance

said that these sparks had been falling all over the planet for hundreds of years and were a gift for humanity, that we would not perceive or experience until we were ready. Then we would realize that this golden reality was already here, that there was no need to reach it, because it was with us.

A moment later, I saw an image of children with golden sparks in their chests. I recognized some of them and understood how important it was that we cared for the sparks that were shining in their hearts. It filled me with hope.

When I returned, I told this to the Shepherdess, and she looked into my eyes and smiled.

"In the last days of the descent," she said, "some children were born who, from an early age, showed a different quality of love and understanding. They were born with an awareness that combined the understanding of the life of the last two world cycles. This made them the precursors of the energy of the next era, the *Great Cycle of Integration*, an age when the conscious development of individuality and innate personal qualities would unite with a clear perception of the interconnection and unity of all life. Only a few precursor-children were born at first, but their number increased with time, and their presence brought a special light into the world.

"A small amount of this light had existed in the planet for millennia; for there were always individuals and small groups of people who had reached this same awareness. Among them, there were even a few who were gifted with an even vaster, infinite quality of love, who became known as masters of unconditional love. They embodied the wisdom and qualities of cycles posterior to the cycle of integration.

"Through their realization and deeds, these masters helped the world. During the descent, they transmitted the principles of love that would flow in the following cycle of integration— the recognition of the relationship among all things and love as a manifestation of a single source, which, at different times and places, had received different names.

"During the descent, these messages were often corrupted,

Hope

twisted, and used to obtain more power over others. However, they carried a special quality unknown to most—golden seeds of infinite love and divine remembrance. So when someone came into contact with the masters of unconditional love or their message, the seeds reached their hearts, became rooted there, and remained in a latent state.

"For some time, most of the seeds slept inside these human hearts. Every so often, some of them sprouted, awakening a desire for freedom, peace, and fellowship. But the day finally came when these seeds began to transform the hearts of many at once. Those who felt this awakening of the heart called it 'inspiration.'

"Inspiration reached people from all walks of life, gradually leading them to cease focusing on what made them different from others, and to begin noticing what they shared in common.

"Thus, a new feeling of belonging to life and a certain sibling love was born in them. It also inflamed their hearts, making them want to share their new feelings with the rest of the world.

"The voices of these inspired individuals were heard in many places. Their message promoted understanding and trust beyond confusion and fear. They shared it in different ways and settings; but it was always recognizable because it transcended differences.

"In time, many people heard the message of the inspired and began to change. It filled them with happiness and hope, as it momentarily removed the distortion of the time. And they, too, wanted to share their new feelings with others.

"As the seeds of infinite love continued to grow, they began to provoke more noticeable changes. In many places, the calls for war ceased, the accumulation of weapons was abandoned, and a friendlier way of communication among nations was sought. Abuse and discrimination decreased. There was a surge of artistic expressions of love, beauty, and solidarity.

Remembrance

"In many people, a caring feeling of responsibility to humanity and the planet surfaced, ways to protect the Earth and her wonders were sought, ways of caring for water and food and quality-of-life for people were implemented.

"During the whole cycle of differentiation, there had been significant scientific advances. From the galactic to the microscopic, research and studies unveiled great secrets of creation. But through the energy of inspiration, the relationships that existed among the different fields of study became more visible, and new integrated disciplines emerged to explore new terrain.

"As time went on, the number of inspired voices continued to grow. Some of the most potent voices came from the precursors, and those who had been raised with their understanding. Each of them, in their way, began to plant this vision of worldwide inter-connectedness in daily life, which brought to light an even more precise understanding of the existing injustices and inequalities. However, this was not enough to end the period of the *Descent*."

With these words, the Shepherdess ended her story, and said that we would continue the following day.

I was crushed. I tried to sleep that night, but could not. My mind was full of distressing thoughts. To hear that the descent would not end, not even with all these changes, caused me much pain. The New Earth seemed increasingly unattainable.

Chapter Twenty-Five
A Change of Course

As soon as the Shepherdess got up in the morning, I did not wait to greet her before telling her of my disappointment: "I was hopeful that the descent would be finishing, that this period in my world was coming to an end. Besides the horrors, I have also witnessed many positive things taking place around me; I have met inspired individuals and precursor children—but this Earth where *you* live seems beyond reach!"

The Shepherdess responded:

"The sprouting of the seeds of infinite love was a gradual awakening of the heart that took longer than one great cycle. This awakening began during the descent with the opening to a new dimension of love, a love beyond oneself, which is not a love without limits, but a step in that direction. However, the distortion became so deep in the last phases of the descent that it created illusions that seduced even the inspired.

"Many fell in love with the power they had achieved, to the point that they confused their personal desires with the actual need of their souls, and offered their own ideas as if they had come from higher regions.

"At the same time, others were also tempted by pride. Some forgot that they had received inspiration as a gift, thinking that it belonged to them, or that they had somehow earned or deserved it. They felt superior to others, and declared themselves to have special powers or qualities, or to be 'chosen,' the very voice of 'the One.' They felt entitled to be heard and enjoyed exercising influence over others, and sought admiration and personal benefit. In so doing, they damaged,

Remembrance

and even corrupted the legacy they had received.

"The greater the understanding, the greater the responsibility. Whoever gains wisdom becomes a door for others. Opening the door to the *Cycle of Integration* was part of the function of the inspired. The seduction created by the distorted reality of the time was a test that they had to endure.

"In the beginning, the energy of interrelatedness within the incoming *Cycle of Integration* appealed to a significant part of the world. However, it soon began to clash with the energy of separation, division, and discrimination that had ruled for thousands of years; the confrontation became stronger and stronger. As the air was saturated with this new vision, the rejection of it grew deeper in some places which held tight to the old vision of the world. Fear of change made many cling to the older structures.

"Meanwhile, the new vision continued growing and expanding around the world. To stop the spread of the new vision, manipulation of every kind was used. Mass media was used to mislead the public and prevent change. People were buried in lies. Wars and destruction, resentment and revenge, bitterness and tragedy followed. There was even an increase in desire for power and domination over others, and people continued abusing and contaminating the planet. Slavery and suffering persisted in all its forms. Nothing changed. It was more of the same."

She stopped speaking and would not talk again till evening.

It gave me time to digest her words. I needed to think. When the sun went down, we sat at the mouth of the cave. Slowly, as the sky filled with stars, the Shepherdess resumed where she had left off.

"During the descent, as a result of this clash between opposing ideas, a chance to leave this period more rapidly was missed, and the increase in confusion produced a regression to the gloomiest parts of that era.

"However, just when things seemed darkest, a light began to shine. Although few noticed it, for just as a mortally wounded

A Change of Course

wild beast lashes out and attacks until its last breaths, so was *Descent* in its death throes.

"The new period in the life of Earth began in a rather unexpected way.

"As the inspired shared their message, they also unknowingly blanketed the Earth with a fine dust, an emanation of the seed of love that had sprouted in their hearts, which was carried in the air and inhaled by people who had not heard the message, or had not been interested in it, or who had even rejected it, leading to a gradual shift in perception. People began to question more and more the reality in which they lived, and increasingly recognized the miseries plaguing the planet. At the same time, there were other factors shifting consciousness and rooting the new cycle.

"One was a change in the mass media. Many of those who controlled the media had used it to misinform people, to alter the truth to support their own points of view and increase their power. But amid the most challenging days of the descent, some media sources began to understand the deeper meaning of their influence and responsibility. They stopped acting as a means of distraction, confusion, and division. Each day, more communicators transmitted honest information that encouraged reflection and the search for real solutions to the problems that affected communities. This shift began to transform people's perception of the world and life.

"Another fundamental transformation took place in the spiritual field. There was a reconciliation among diverse religions and traditions, which discovered that they had more in common than they had previously believed. Thus, there was a slow building of understanding and acceptance, based on the recognition of similarities in scripture and their shared desire for the health of humanity, the search for truth, and the building of an internal connection with the source. Some spiritual leaders realized that they had been preaching what they themselves were unable to do, or had not tried. Thus, they once again sought to emulate the examples of the great beings whose teachings they followed.

Remembrance

"Increasingly the old ideas and ways of understanding life began to fade naturally, and an opportunity arose for the development of deep communion."

Chapter Twenty-Six
Time to Come Back

The Ageless Woman returned the evening of the following day. The Shepherdess invited us to her home. The time at the grotto had ended.

We left the cave and walked in the direction of the town. I was walking at my own pace, a few steps behind, and from time to time, stopped to observe the night's scenery. The light of the moon, accompanied by the evening star, illuminated our path.

Finally, I, too, could see a light in the midst of the darkness and the suffering of the world in which I lived.

While walking, my heart began to beat vigorously. The heartbeats spread throughout my entire body. They permeated the air I breathed and the ground upon which I walked. Like the constant waves of the rising tide, they reached the Ageless Woman and the Shepherdess, and spread to the town and the waters of the river. They went up to the moon and the evening star and the other heavenly bodies twinkling in the sky. Everything was beating. The whole of creation was a single heart, beating—my heart.

The Shepherdess lived in a cabin surrounded by bushes and trees. The ceiling of the great room had a skylight through which the moon could be seen. Looking at it, I fell asleep and had a dream.

I was in a town surrounded by children playing, people walking about and talking. It was a clean town, with flowers hanging from the windows of the buildings. Observing the

Remembrance

people come and go, I was taken by a sense of humility and realized that this feeling was coming from them. I could feel that these people were awake in a very particular way.

Across the street was a large stone building, taller than the rest. It was a library. I crossed to it and entered the building. The first thing I saw was a book, which I opened. There were some beautiful drawings and illustrations in it with descriptions. The book told the story of the people of that town. As I began to read the book, it became immediately apparent that I had not been mistaken regarding them.

The book described two interconnected tests that they had overcome: the test of singularity and equality, and the test of power. They comprehended that every individual thing in existence was a unique expression of the divine; and at the same time, that all things were one and the same. As a result, they were able to keep in check their personal desires to control others; and as their understanding deepened, this desire fell away entirely.

The book also told of how they had reached a new level of consciousness infused with a love that embraced everything and everyone. This love had given them a wisdom beyond ideas and ideals, and beyond the mere awareness of the interrelation of all existence, which allowed them to live consciously with a deep sense of the unity of life and the love from which all things were made.

From one page to the next, I read the names of individual bearers of remembrance and the story of the New Earth. It said that they had felt a common call to help awaken those who needed and wanted to awaken. However, they did not feel called to share their understanding in the same way as the inspired ones. Instead, these bearers of remembrance felt called to lead a simple life, remaining open and receptive to the seekers who might come to them.

Transmitting the knowing that lived in their hearts, for them, was not about teaching anyone, but about sharing through the example of their lives, through their being and actions. They

Time to Come Back

understood that their function was to love unconditionally and live from the wisdom of the soul. Often, they used stories, legends, and poems to reach the hearts of the people who came to them, telling their truth as they knew it; they did not lie or try to convince anyone of anything.

The bearers of remembrance lived as directed by their souls, in accord with the spirit of life. They gave themselves entirely, without expecting anything in return, because the freedom they knew was a freedom ignored by most. Their experience of freedom caused them to commit themselves to helping others to achieve it. They realized that each human being had an inborn right to discover their own path to wholeness and the source. For this reason, they did not establish spiritual movements, hierarchies, or systems of belief. Instead, they shared their experiences and knowledge, ensuring that others would remain completely free of them.

Generation after generation, the world became increasingly populated with bearers of remembrance, until the whole of humanity remembered.

The sunlight through the skylight woke me up. My heart was full. I felt honored to be shown this book, and of being with these two women, in this place, in this New Earth.

That morning, the three of us went for a walk. We crossed the town and reached a field of clovers. I was walking distractedly when I saw a four-leaf clover. The Shepherdess said it was *sign;* I should pick it and keep it.

We continued walking until we reached the top of the hill where my journey had begun. The music of the New Earth sounded loud in my ears. As I looked at the valley and the town below, I realized how much this place had changed me. In a way, I was a new woman.

Remembrance

"Today," said the Ageless Woman holding my hand, "our time together comes to an end."

I felt dizzy; I was not really ready for these words.

"It's time; you have a job to do; the story of our journey is not just for you."

Without knowing what to say, I only asked whether I would see them again.

"Maybe we'll meet again, maybe we won't," the Ageless Woman answered. "It does not matter: we have *been* together, we *are* together, and we *will be* together in the heart."

"Take the clover with you as a remembrance," said the Shepherdess, "and tell this story; do not forget any of it."

I did not want to leave; but deep inside, I knew it was time.

The three of us held hands, looked into each other's eyes, and then leaned our heads together, closing our eyes. I felt that our union included more than ourselves, much more. The New Earth and all of her nature, the jungle of metamorphosis, the angels, the town and its people, were also present. I felt infinitely sad and infinitely grateful.

"Thank you," I whispered. "I am so grateful for all you have taught me . . . for everything."

A fragrance of flowers came from somewhere; I felt love in the air. In that moment, in my mind, the Earth appeared, turning silently in space, and the garment of remembrance floating beside it.

The suit became more and more transparent and ethereal until only the golden strand remained visible. This strand formed a delicate web of gold, expanding until it enveloped and covered the world completely. Then the web slowly entered the body of the planet, permeating it with its splendor, until the Earth was transformed into a golden star.

The radiance continued increasing, dissolving and making subtler the visible body of the star-world, until it too became ethereal, like the garment of remembrance, and became a crystalline star of the invisible universes.

Part Six:
The Doors of Memory

Chapter Twenty-Seven
After the Visions

Toward the end of July 1997, the teachings came to an end. Freezing, rainy days had turned into humid summer warmth. Although my daily life continued, full of the same chores, activities, and outings with my children and husband, there was a shift in me—I could no longer see the world or myself as before.

The magic, the shine, and the music of the visions stayed with me, as did the unitive consciousness of my soul, which began to infuse my everyday perception. Matter and spirit became one. My reality kept losing materiality, becoming mainly energy.

I was still unable to sleep more than a few hours each night due to the energy flowing through my body. I seemed to have lost the roots that held me to this world. It felt as if I were naked, without clothes separating me from the exterior.

I remained open and clairvoyant without any desire or intention on my part. I read the unconscious, minds, hearts, and souls of whoever crossed my path like open books. My mind was overloaded with the intimacies of people I met in passing. In some ways, I became a kind of magnet for people's greatest secrets.

My sensitivity became so heightened that we had to move to a less populated area. We rented a house outside of town. I reduced my social interactions and devoted myself mainly to raising our children. I also attended to the intense need I had to dive inside myself, to know more and more deeply the new woman I had become. I found refuge in contemplation.

Remembrance

When the school year started, and the twins began pre-kindergarten in the morning, I found some space to look at the notes in my diary. I spent time alone in nature observing, listening, smelling.

On those walks, I felt protected and embraced by the love of Mother Earth, by her perfume, power, intelligence, beauty, and wisdom. I fell in love with nature, with her infinite femininity. She rejuvenated me. Deep meaning and a miraculous sense of oneness permeated my life.

But that miracle lived in a place too intimate inside me. Even when I shared it in-part with my children and my husband, it was still secret.

Although I was fully aware that I was to transmit the teaching that I had been given, I did not know how to do this for many years.

That same summer, my godmother came to visit us and brought me a few of the books I had requested months before. I began to read them with interest. There, I found the first explanations of what I had experienced. Even so, I continued to struggle to find the words to describe what had happened to me. When I attempted to explain, the responses I often received led me to feel still more intimidated by the idea of having to share any teaching of this feminine wisdom.

For a time, the fear of being criticized or ridiculed was so deep that, although in my heart I knew that what I had lived was real, my mind would doubt and question it.

I felt torn by fears that paralyzed me, and by other fears of failing to do what had been asked of me. Finally, I realized that 'communicating the teachings' was not about repeating what I had heard, describing what I had seen, or explaining this vision of life, but about making the teaching my own. Only when I achieved this in my own life, would it be time to share these teachings.

To be able to do this, I needed to re-examine my culture's view of feminine wisdom and its consequences. This was an extremely painful period in my life. Ironically, as I became

After the Visions

aware of how interconnected the whole of life was, I felt completely isolated.

Looking back, however, I see how the potency of the pain, and the feeling of loneliness, eventually became an engine that gave me the strength to grow the roots I needed, to learn to moderate my sensitivity and confront my fear.

My Own Search

Soon after my husband Walter finished law school, we moved to a rural area north of San Francisco. The years of bucolic life passed quickly. We decided to homeschool our children. This approach to their education required hours of hard work each day, but also gave us the freedom to travel at any time of the year. Despite being quite busy, I still found the time to satisfy my thirst for inner growth.

While still living in Virginia, I had met a renowned British-born Sufi mystic and Jungian psychologist specializing in dream interpretation, meditation, and the *anima mundi* (the soul of the world); and since our arrival to northern California, I had begun to study at his center. There I received an in-depth preparation in the analysis of dreams and spiritual experiences and found in the teachings of the *anima mundi* a message similar to the one of my vision.

I also expanded my spiritual knowledge through a deeper study of sacred texts, mystical Christianity and Sufism, finding better words for communicating what I had lived in my visions.

For seven years, I went through a period of retreat, where the education of my children, the care of my family, and the cultivation of my inner life through reading, study, meditation, and contemplation, occupied all of my days.

Toward the middle of this time, I was asked to translate the books and web pages of the Sufi center into Spanish, and to respond to the inquiries they received in Spanish. I was also encouraged to write the visions and teachings of the feminine wisdom down in a book, but I did not yet feel I was ready to do so.

Remembrance

After finishing a spiritual counseling course, this period of retreat slowly concluded. I started to work with women and couples. I developed a project called Essential Oneness: A Feminine Wisdom *(La Unidad Esencial: Sabiduría Femenina)*, and began to organize women's circles and to write and give talks on feminine wisdom.

Sometime later, the Sufi center asked me to bring its teachings and meditative practices to my home in South America. From then on, I spent some months each year traveling through various countries, where I lectured and taught courses in universities and institutes, formed study-groups, and led retreats and workshops on the mystical path, meditation, dream studies, oneness, and spiritual ecology. In 2014, my autobiography, *El Llamado de Mi Corazón* (The Call of My Heart) was published in Spanish.

During this period, I was approached again and again, particularly by women, to talk about the wisdom of the feminine, her spirituality, her connection to the soul and the Earth, and her language in the oneiric or dream world. Responding to this need, my talks and writing on this theme increased. I completed an interspiritual mentoring course, through which I hoped to integrate the tradition of the feminine wisdom among the mystical traditions and spiritual paths. Little by little, this work required more of my time, until it became my primary teaching. Today, I understand that all those years of study and inner work were necessary to find the words, the tone, and sense of what had been transmitted to me.

The Damage of Patriarchy

We live in a generally patriarchal culture which ignores and denies the true nature of the feminine. This culture is a distortion of the 'sacred masculine' into what has been called 'toxic masculinity.' The influence of this patriarchal culture is so pervasive that it affects almost every aspect of our lives today and thus requires systemic change.

After the Visions

The mythology of ancient cultures and many of our sacred texts expose the roots of patriarchy, whose values have defined and framed the reality-system of the western world for millennia.

In Greek myth, the goddess Athena was born from the head of Zeus, her father, after he ate his wife, Metis. In this way, Zeus stole the capacity to give birth from the feminine, and in doing so, created a warrior goddess with strength and independence, but separated from the greatest power of her being.

Similarly, the biblical story of creation is an account without childbirth or childhood, where the first woman comes from the rib of a man, and both are created as adults by God, the father. Likewise, the immaculate conception of Mary (born without sin), the virgin birth of her son, and her ascent to heaven, have placed the feminine in an unreachable category, far beyond the grasp of any human woman.

Among the most significant harms are those suffered by 'Eve.' In older Christian art, we find depictions of the Temptation and the Fall.

In these, Satan, in the form of the serpent, acquires more and more feminine traits, until, becoming woman, transforming into Eve herself, taking a face and torso identical to hers. At the same time, Adam's appearance becomes progressively naive, innocent and inoffensive.

Bugiardini, Guiliano di Piero di Simone. *Adam; Eve*. 1475–1554. Metropolitan Museum of Art, New York, USA.

Remembrance

These works tell us how this myth was distorted over time, justifying Adam and demonizing Eve, making her implicitly culpable for the expulsion from Eden and humanity's fall from grace (even though it was Adam whom God had forbidden to eat from the tree of the knowledge of good and evil before the serpent appeared and Eve "tempted" him).

Eve and the Serpent. *The Furtmeyr Bible.*

Thus, 'wickedness' has been projected onto woman, making her a symbol of betrayal and deceit, and of sinful seduction. This negative attribution has also been used to justify mistreatment and abuse of women, and legitimized the imposition of unjust impediments and prohibitions on them.

In the same way, the Earth, the great feminine body, became a place of exile for the feminine soul, a place of utility without sacred value, instead of an Edenic paradise.

We live in a world that has forgotten its true story, in a distorted myth that disregards the wisdom of the feminine. In our society, Earth is no longer the mother whose love gives us a home and all that we need to live. A woman's maternity—that gift that unites the past, present, and future, that exists in her and allows us to host a soul, the most sacred gift to the planet—is seen as little more than a biological function. The knowledge that women, just as they conceive a child, can conceive a new world and a new humanity, has been obscured.

The Opportunity for a New Cycle

The message delivered to me and inscribed in this book is not just for women, but for the feminine that exists in us all—women, men, and those who exist in the liminal spaces of gender identity, too—because the feminine is awakening and

After the Visions

tearing down, more and more forcefully, the curtains of the reality constructed by patriarchy. The return of the feminine is unstoppable; our bodies (and the bodies of women, in particular) feel the power of her re-emergence.

The cycle of differentiation brought with it an energy of separation that favored the development and expansion of masculine qualities in the world, in both men and women. But it also gave birth to patriarchy, which degenerated into the abuse of the feminine that we now recognize.

The feminine is a unifying force, a force of integration. Her awakening is reconnecting us with Mother Earth, whom we refer to again, as in the old days, by the name of the goddess Gaia. This new cycle has started to dilute the more artificial, culturally established divisions between masculine and feminine roles, and to rekindle the feminine qualities in all human beings.

This same force is making the mother-father, the friend, the lover, the companion, the woman-man, who works in the outer world, and the one who works in the home, into a unified person. We are all being called to live our wholeness fully, to integrate our feminine and masculine qualities.

It can be challenging to live the many facets and dimensions of the feminine: the subtlety, the power and strength, the integration, fluidity and perseverance, the receptivity, fertility and sensitivity, the tenderness, dynamism and sensuality, the intuition, generosity and intensity. There is also the capacity for attraction, creation, transformation and contentment, flexibility, compassion, and wisdom. It is even more difficult to live these qualities in a world that has divided us, that has cut femininity into pieces and hidden her true nature.

This may be why we experience a deep pain when facing the harm that continues to be inflicted on the Earth, on women, and on the feminine qualities in all human beings. Something cries out in us when we see the devastation of forests, the contamination of waters, the extinction of species. We are filled with grief each time we sense the suffering of the world due to the wrongs that are perpetrated against the defenseless

Remembrance

and forgotten. It is a sadness that feels like loss and causes mourning. It connects us with our compassion, born from shared suffering. This cry of the heart is a prayer for healing and renovation, and at the same time, a call to action.

But in its place, sometimes there arises an abhorrence so deep that it freezes the heart and disconnects us from it. It is a vengeful loathing, difficult to hold, which frequently appears without our full understanding of the locus from which it arises. This feeling is a poison that does not originate in the feminine, but has adhered to her over time. It is a hatred for having been degraded and exploited for thousands of years, a hatred that was kept repressed, that could not be expressed openly, but that neither forgets nor forgives, and which seeks reprisals.

Meanwhile, from everywhere, we receive the message that women need to know their value and live it, that they need to empower themselves and express the totality of who they are in the world, that they need to regain their power and manifest it in themselves, within the family and outside the family, in the larger society and in the working world. It is indeed indispensable that women do this; but we need to empower ourselves in the feminine way, not patriarchally, or through this ancient rancor that arises uncontrolled, hurting us and everything it touches.

How do we do this when patriarchal culture has caused us forget the deeper meaning of the feminine? When it destroyed the mirrors that reflect her back to us? When it has made us all, in a certain way, to greater and lesser degrees, patriarchal? When many of us have become Athena to empower ourselves, without realizing that the goddess is a product of a patriarchal myth?

In order to be accepted and acceptable, this culture has devalued and divided the feminine, degrading our intuitive wisdom and our bodies, and even one another.

Today, we live in this paradox.

Chapter Twenty-Eight
The Rebirth of the Feminine

The feminine is not re-emerging to take us back to the past. Nor is it seeking to punish or claim reparations. The rebirth of the feminine has a deeper purpose. The feminine we have forgotten is a divine essence: it is the power of love made into a substance which took the form of creation, of everything created.

The feminine is re-emerging to give birth to a higher consciousness, a more embracing love that might bring an end to this time of imbalance in the world. It could be said that the feminine has come to unite with the masculine, and from their union, a child will be born—a new consciousness and greater love.

Although some aspects of this new consciousness and greater love are already manifesting in the world, and the feminine qualities are being expressed more strongly each day, the sacred meaning of the feminine (and the deeper change that this meaning can produce on Earth) are still at risk of getting lost. The union may not materialize, or may dissolve, and the child's growth may yet cease.

This consciousness, like all newborns, needs to be protected and cared for until it is strong enough to flourish on its own. The current cultural distortion and forgetfulness, added to thousands of years of patriarchal abuse and devaluation of the feminine and the vengeful rancor it has spawned, threaten this development.

Thus, we need to *remember* the message of the feminine, the power of love incarnate. When we remember, the world will remember.

Remembrance

If we fail to do this, the re-emergence of the feminine will be just another cycle of greater forgetfulness that will trample the healthy roots of a possible future.

As her representatives, women have a very particular role to play. Many of the virtues of the feminine have been rejected and destroyed by patriarchy. Thus, we learn from an early age that we are 'not enough,' that we are always lacking something, whether beauty or intelligence or something else. The spiritual meaning of the womb and the primordial quality of the feminine has been corrupted, attacked, and buried. We were robbed of a fundamental part of our dignity.

That part is our essential purity.

It was during a spiritual gathering that I learned about this. In a book I read a passage that claimed that women were as pure as gold, and that this purity could never be tainted. This idea impacted me deeply; but try as I might, I could not believe it.

The visions showed me that this purity is real: it is the essence of the feminine, of the Earth, the natural world, and the soul.

I had always seen this purity in my children, and when working with children in the classroom. But I did not feel it in myself. The denial and forgetfulness of this quality had marked me deeply.

Only after a long period of introspection did I begin to understand that this purity was actually an integral part of my being, and I was able to experience it. This was a great liberation.

The human soul is so subtle that it could never come into the world through a vehicle that is not as pure as itself. The feminine essence of life, soul, and body, is a 'womb,' and it is as pure as the spirit of life that inhabits it. This essential purity is always virginal, untouched, and immaculate. No one can give it to us; nor can we develop or evoke it. It simply *Is*.

We need to remember this purity, because it does not only exist to give birth to a soul. This essence can also allow us to

The Rebirth of the Feminine

bring life and meaning to everything we touch, to everything we look at, if we look and touch with love.

Purity relates to the recognition of the sacredness of all life and the unity of existence: the very mystery of creation.

Our reconnection with our essential purity and the sacredness of all things can bring about the return of a new world cycle of the feminine that awakens in us her qualities and gives back to the world its lost meaning.

This has always been the importance of woman.

For me, the visions came to open the door to the remembrance of this sacred meaning, so that we may re-discover the fact that we are links in a chain that unites our purpose with the purpose of the universe, so that we may know that we are indispensable to creating a better future.

Experiencing the gift of our purity is the goal. It is the gift that we can give to ourselves and to the world in this time of unfathomable suffering.

To recover our sense of purity may demand patience and perseverance. We may need to take small, certain steps as we remove the blindfold and retrace the path that led us into forgetfulness.

We may need to bring into the light the patriarchal notions that hide in our thinking, feeling, and acting.

With our love, our remembrance, and our purpose aligned with the cosmos, we can conceive a new day. We can give birth to the New Earth.

What is the task ahead? To remember that our physical nature, and our divine essence, are eternally united; to recognize the invincible power of life that beats inside us; to recover the incorruptible purity of matter; to connect with the joy of life; to respect ourselves; to work for the rights of all human beings; to heal the Earth; to believe once again that love conquers all; and to embrace the sacredness of our bodies.

Part Seven:
Teachings of a Feminine Spirituality

Love

The Earth is infinitely large in comparison to the individual beings that inhabit her, and her love is scaled accordingly, infinitely large in comparison to our own. The Earth's love was so immense and inclusive from the beginning that we (and all the other individual beings of the planet) could not contain it. Thus, nature assists us, holding that vast love in place, while helping us to experience and express it progressively in our evolution. The incorporation and experience of infinite love is a continual process that proceeds from the close and specific—the love for oneself—to the furthest and most embracing, universal love; from the protection of oneself to the protection of all life.

The Care of the Earth

The bliss and peace of Earth are under the care of her protecting angel, and a group of angelic beings assisting that angel. They preserve the fundamental notes and qualities that support the well-being of the planet. Other angels care for its creatures, tending to and guiding the different realms of nature.

There are also non-angelic beings that participate in the care of nature. Throughout the life of the planet, the elementals were among the best known of them. They help plants, animals, minerals, and other creations in the natural realm.

The Evolution of the Earth

In the evolutionary narrative of the Earth, all life on the planet (not only humanity) has been transitioning from Moon to Sun, from the unconscious to the conscious, from the collective to the individual. It is a developmental necessity.

Both the era of lunar supremacy and the era of solar supremacy have fulfilled their purpose and completed their function. Now comes the cycle of the Earth, the Cosmic Earth. In this new era, the influences of Moon and Sun are waning. Their forces are uniting and forming a triangle of power and love with the planet, which gives birth to a new world.

This birth first takes place in the heart of humanity and the planet, the rest of planetary life following.

The Present Moment

The present moment is outside of time.

Living outside of time is a different reality. Outside of time, there is neither past nor future. In that sense, when one lives in the present moment, it is always new.

There is a difference between living in the present moment consciously and unconsciously. Living consciously in it is a particular state of being, part of the consciousness of the soul. Almost all life on Earth lives in the present without consciousness of time; it lives in the present without knowing it. Children, when they are very young, also live unknowingly in the present moment; only as they grow do they begin to develop a conscious awareness of linear time, of past and future. The more the temporal reality prevails, the more the present moment gets lost.

Teachings of a Feminine Spirituality

Angels

Angels are forces, energies, qualities of divinity; their temperament defines their quality, and this quality defines their mission and function.

When they have to communicate, they focus their attention on the message and the receiver is granted a rare vision, dream, experience, or aural message. However, this is not an independent action; angelic beings can only intervene directly in human affairs when it is the divine will that they do so.

In their way, angels can see and hear human beings; and when humans call on them, they can assist if it is the will of God.

The specific mission of each angelic order is not determined by human will or desire, but by divine will. Their only function is to fulfill that will, which is often predetermined.

They neither want to be venerated, nor should they be.

Other non-angelic beings can be mistaken for angels. However, they do seek to be venerated and fulfill a variety of human requests. They seek repayment for their favors at the time of a person's physical transition.

The Porous Layers of Existence

It could be said that existence is made of layers. Each layer is an eco-system, a universe in itself, but its borders are porous, allowing for the passing from one layer to another.

Water and air are two of these layers. The aquatic world and the world on dry land are different; each one has its own characteristics and offers a particular form of life. But they are also permeable and seep into each other and mix where they

Remembrance

touch. The whiteness of the foam in waves is air in the water, and clouds in the sky are water in the air. So we see that two levels of existence, which can seem so far apart, are actually intertwined and porous.

When one inhabits one of the layers or planes of existence, one perceives and experiences life through that particular layer's reality. However, if one gets closer to the edge of that plane, one begins to perceive elements of the next reality. The world of everyday reality is different from the world of dreams, but when one rests, one can experience the nearness of both worlds, how they intermix, and what they have in common.

Like all planes of existence, the layer of the non-physical universe and the physical universe also have porous borders. They have 'passages' through which angels and other beings of the subtle planes can enter and exist, accessing material reality.

For human beings, the moment of physical death is a door to the non-physical realm. Other doors connect their reality with the ethereal worlds during their life on the planet.

There are many other access doors in the human being that put them in contact with other planes. The borders of the planes of the mind, the emotions and the physical body interconnect; that is why thoughts, feelings, and bodily sensations often influence each other. Other doors join the personal with the collective. Also, some relate one individual with another and their energies mix.

If a person is too porous—if their doors are wide open—it is necessary to limit access to the opening, as the mix of realities can confuse them.

On the other hand, when the connection between planes is obstructed or difficult to establish, it is necessary to develop or train the 'organs' that sense the connection to other realities, just as aquatic beings were once challenged to modify their bodies for living on dry land.

And there are particular 'doors' that it is best not to open or pass.

Teachings of a Feminine Spirituality

The Created and the Uncreated, The One and the Many

The single essence, the source, the whole or divinity, is eternal, infinite, omniscient, and almighty. It is one, alone, and indivisible; and yet, it also has created aspects—*creation*—and uncreated aspects—*nothingness*. Its self-division in the created and the uncreated is and is not. The division of the created aspect into an infinite multiplicity of creations also is and is not.

Divinity is the essence, the origin of everything that exists and does not exist; and it is also the form that the essence takes, and the way in which it expresses. The divine, ultimate truth, is beyond existence and non-existence.

The created and the uncreated are like the body and spirit of divinity. Body and spirit are inseparable because nothing can be outside the whole.

The soul is the intersection between the uncreated spirit and the physical body. So divinity is a ternary unit (composed of three things) and a unitary trinity. In unity, there are no opposites. Everything, something, and nothing are the same. Everything is spirit. Everything is nothingness.

Born in Cordoba, Argentina, Alejandra Warden is an educator, interspiritual teacher, and counselor. Founder of the Essential Oneness Feminine Wisdom Project, she offers talks, workshops, and retreats on the sacred feminine, dream interpretation, meditation, eco-spirituality, interspirituality, mystical Christianity and Sufism in the United States and South America. She currently lives with her husband in Washington State.

www.ingramcontent.com/pod-product-compliance
Lightning Source LLC
Chambersburg PA
CBHW030115240426
43673CB00028B/482/J